IRISH CUSTOMS
AND BELIEFS

IRISH CUSTOMS
AND BELIEFS

KEVIN DANAHER

MERCIER PRESS
IRISH PUBLISHER – IRISH STORY

MERCIER PRESS
Cork
www.mercierpress.ie

© Kevin Danaher 1964
This edition 2004
ScandBook AB, Sweden

ISBN: 978 1 85635 442 4

10 9 8 7 6 5 4 3 2

A CIP record for this title is available from the British Library

Printed and bound by ScandBook AB in the EU.

CONTENTS

❖ Wandering People

Once upon a time there was a Corkman who vowed that he would never rest until he reached the end of the world. And so he travelled many a weary mile over land and over sea, until finally he came to a great wall that reached nearly to the sky. Up he went from crevice to crevice with his heart in his mouth until, at the very top, he found a Kerryman calmly seated, smoking his pipe and gazing wistfully into the infinite space beyond. A slight exaggeration perhaps; he may have been smoking a cigarette, but the fact remains that the Irish have always been notable travellers. A continental scholar, Walafrid Strabo, who flourished eleven hundred years ago, remarked that the Irish of his time were so given to wandering abroad that it was second nature to them. He had seen them come by the shipload, monks and craftsmen and scholars, 'a whole herd of philosophers' as one contemporary put it, who were made welcome by kings and bishops and left their mark deep on religion and learning in Europe. And, as we might expect, there were others, less welcome perhaps to the kings and the bishops, but loved by the ordinary people, jugglers, minstrels and poets, experts in the arts of entertainment for which the Irish were noted. There were some who scorned the easy roads of France and Germany and turned their ships westward and northward where they certainly discovered Iceland and possibly reached what is now America, and returned to tell of the great ice islands which floated on the sea, and the tusked walrus and the sprouting whales and the strange and wonderful adventures which befell them in the magic islands of the great ocean.

We can be sure that there were Irishmen out and about long before the great days of the missionaries. King Dáithí is said to have been killed by lightning at the foot of the Alps, and Irish raiders snatched Patrick into slavery and, all unknown to

themselves, changed history for Ireland and for Europe. Of these
earlier wanderers we know hardly anything, nor are we ever
likely to know much. But since St Colmcille turned his back
on his beloved Derry to go into God's exile we can follow the
course of the endless stream of Irishmen to the ends of the earth.
Of the saints and the soldiers we have heard most; we all know
the names of Columbanus and Fiachra and Killian, of Sarsfield
and Lally and O'Mahony. But there is hardly a spot on the globe
where an Irish foot has not trod, from the Polar wastes to the
jungles of central Africa and from the cannibal islands to the
palaces of the kings.

With such a tradition of wandering we may well imagine
that people were moving about the home island too. We often
have the quite mistaken idea that people 'long ago' lived in a sort
of remote isolation, never moving out of their own parish and
seldom seeing a stranger. Far different was the true state of affairs,
for with all our hikers and all our motor cars, it is probable that
there are less people moving on the Irish roads now than there
were at almost any time in the past. For one thing, travel is too
fast nowadays; getting to the destination as fast as possible is what
interests most of us. In the old days it was different; the journey
was interesting and exciting of itself, and the wise traveller set
himself out to enjoy every minute of it. Besides that there were
many classes of people whose livelihood depended upon their
moving from place to place. Take, for instance, the bands of
poets who imposed themselves on the populace, eating a chief
or noble out of house and home and then passing on to the next
hospitable house with their extravagant demands for bigger and
better hospitality, calling for fresh fruit in the dead of winter and
demanding comfortable beds, each with a second bed at a slightly
lower level, in case they fell out during the night! If anyone
refused their demands they composed satires on him – funny and
malicious songs that were spread about so that they were sung by
every scullion and cattleboy in the country, to the eternal shame
of the victim. Think of the band that descended on Guaire, the

good king of Connaught, over six hundred poets, their womenfolk and servants, and a hundred and fifty hounds. Lucky for him that his brother, St Marbhán, was there to help him, for although his wealth was great and his generosity proverbial, the demands of the poets were entirely unreasonable. Cuckoos to sing to them between Big and Little Christmas was one of their minor requests. No wonder that the men of Ireland rose against them in the end and would have driven them out of the country, bag and baggage, but for the intervention of another saint, Colmcille, who begged permission for them to stay, under promise of good behaviour. But for centuries after this, and even down to our own day, the wandering poets have been on the roads of Ireland. To some the desire to wander came suddenly, as happened to the scholar Mac Con Glinne: 'A great longing seized the mind of the scholar, to follow poetry and to abandon the studies, for wretched to him was a life overshadowed by study. This came into his mind on a Saturday evening at Roscommon, where he was studying. So he sold what little things he had for two wheaten cakes and a cut of old bacon with a streak across the middle, which he put in his book-bag. And he shaped for himself on the same night a pair of shoes of seven thicknesses of soft leather.' Just like that, and set out next day on his travels, to wind up by saving the king of Munster from a hunger demon and so gaining fame and riches. How many Leaving Cert. students are his brothers in spirit! Then there were not the poor scholars, who travelled in search of learning and not, like Mac Con Glinne, to get away from it. In the Penal times, when it was not easy to get a higher education, there were many poor scholars on the road. If one of them heard of a good teacher, a priest or a hedge-schoolmaster famous for Latin and Greek, he made his way to the parish where the teacher lived and began to study under him, working for a farmer, or teaching the ABC to the farmer's children for his keep. Many are the stories of the poor scholars, and many a poor scholar rose high in the Church or in the service of foreign kings.

There were wandering musicians and ballad singers who

went from fair to fair sure of a night's hospitality because of their art. Some of them were notable people, like the great Turloch Ó Carolan, the 'Last of the Bards', who was a wonderful harper and composer of many fine tunes. He and his like were made welcome at the houses of the gentry, not only the nobles of the old Irish stock but the newer landowners settled by Cromwell and King William of Orange, for anybody who did not at least pretend to be a lover of music was looked on as a boor, be he gentle or simple. There were many notable pipers too and the fashionable gentlemen learned to play the pipes from them – there is a fine set which belonged to Lord Edward Fitzgerald in the National Museum. There were travelling storytellers, and they, too, were sure of a welcome. We all have heard the tale of the poor simple fellow who had no song or story and so was refused lodging at every house – until he came to the house of a man who was in league with 'them that does be in it'. The poor boy was given a bed, but he slept little for he spent the whole night in terror from corpses, coffins, graves and threats of terrible men. Came the morning, and the man of the house said, in a kindly way, 'Now, boy, you'll never again be refused a lodging, for you have a fine long story to tell after the night.'

In several places abroad ancient objects of fine Irish gold or bronze work have been found and fine pieces of foreign origin have turned up in Ireland. Some archaeologists believe that these were made by skilled craftsmen who wandered around from one rich patron to another making fine ornaments and jewellery for good pay. At a later time, within the memory of our grandparents there were many craftsmen on the roads, journeymen coopers, smiths, carpenters, saddlers, shoemakers, stonemasons and many others. Tailors came and stayed in the farmhouse until all the clothes needed by the family were made, then they passed on to the next farmhouse. Wherever there was a big house or a church being built, you might see travelling stonemasons arriving and greeting the chief mason in the secret language of the craft. '*Airig a coistiriú!*' ('a travelling mason!') '*Muintria airig! Coistrig, éis!*'

('God bless you, mason, come in, boy!') but *'is earpach gaid na fearbai sead ó chuí'*, faraway cows have long horns, and before very long the mason might be on the road again towards another job. Sculptors and stone cutters went from job to job in the same way.

Another big section of the wandering people was made up of the *spailpíní*, the migratory labourers who came from the western counties into Leinster, East Munster and East Ulster. In the spring they came with the long spades over their shoulders, and in the harvest with their scythes and reaping hooks. Often they went to the same farmer every year, and the sons went to the same farms to which their fathers had gone. Many of them crossed over to England and Scotland year after year, son after father, to the same farms where their strength and skill and their music and merriment were highly valued and are still remembered. The journey was not without its dangers. An old newspaper of the year 1790 tells how, on the third of August, twenty-seven poor harvesters who were waiting for their ship at the Pigeon House in Dublin Harbour were taken by the press-gang and forced to join the British Navy. The officer in charge of the press-gang remarked airily that if they were going to mow hay they might as well be employed mowing down the king's enemies.

In the bad times there were forlorn little groups of people – a family or two, perhaps – who had been evicted by some harsh landlord and were 'walking before them' to a seaport on their way to America, and coming, shamefaced, to the farmer's door, to ask for a little help on the way. Of course nobody refused them help, and often it was given unasked; the poor evicted people were met by a child of the house or a servant-boy and told to come on up to the house. Of course there were others on the road who were little troubled by any sense of shame, hardened beggars and tramps, but even these seldom met with a refusal, for alms asked in the name of God were given in the name of God, and a Commission of Enquiry into the State of the Poor in the 1830s discovered that the farmers of Ireland gave away in charity each year produce up to the value of *one million pounds*.

One class of wanderers is still going strong, our friends the tinkers, or 'travellers' as they prefer to call themselves. Originally the name was given only to the tinsmiths or whitesmiths who travelled around plying their trade, but at the present very few of the 'travellers' are real tinsmiths at all. Mostly they are pedlars and traders, buying and selling, swapping and borrowing. Nowadays they have caravans and some have motor cars, whereas formerly a spring-cart was sufficient, and earlier still their only means of travel was shank's mare, carrying their 'budgets' and other bundles on their backs. The traditional pattern of movement is kept up; each group or family has its recognised circuit and others will not trespass on it. So we have the same family turning up in one place season after season. They have recognised camping places – recognised, unfortunately, at the first glance, for they are very careless and untidy, and the scattered remains of fires, the tufts of straw, the battered old tins and discarded rags are all too evident. And many a farmer mutters and growls at the mention of the tinkers, remembering broken fences and trampled meadows and heads of cabbage or chickens mysteriously missing. But, against that, the tinkers are a hardy, carefree crew, untouched by the responsibilities and restrictions which afflict those who live in houses and must show a clean face and a respectable habit to the world. And in former times the tinker was a useful, even necessary, craftsman, making and mending household utensils. Even yet the tinsmith holds himself superior to all other travellers, and still keeps up the old secret language of his craft, the 'Tinkers' Cant' which is quite different from *Béarlagar na Saor*, the masons' language. 'A treep of scotchelpy and a nerk of inoc libish' means 'a drink of tea and a bit of sugar'; 'I'm corib with the cloarus' is 'I'm starved with the hunger'. The 'travellers' proudly claim to be of old Irish descent, not in any way connected with the gypsies or any such foreign people. Typical tinker names are Ward, Joyce and MacDonagh in Connaught; Coffey, Carty and O'Brien in Munster; Cash, Doyle and Delaney in Leinster and MacCann, Doherty and Keenan in Ulster. Many of them were, and some still are, notable musicians, fiddlers and pipers, and any old-time musician will remember the Delaneys, the Dorans and the Cashes in this connection.

There are signs that these, the last of the wandering people, may soon be gone from the roads of Ireland, and that only their memory, like that of the journeymen, the *spailpíní* and the poor scholars, will for a time remain. They, like their predecessors, have no place on the modern motorway, but much of the romance and adventure of the road will have died with them.

❖ STAND AND DELIVER!

A visitor to Dublin with an hour or two on his hands might do
worse than go into the National Library and ask to see some
of the old newspapers of two hundred years or so ago, for their
yellowing pages give a curious picture of the comings and goings
of the time. Among other things he will see that they are full
of accounts of highway robberies, and he need not be surprised
to find mention of travellers asking for and getting escorts of
dragoons or coaches advertised as bulletproof. Even the most
frequented roads were not safe. One of busiest roads in Ireland
at the time was the high road from Dublin through Drogheda
and Dundalk to Belfast, and a favourite haunt of highwaymen
was the stretch between the Cat and Cage Inn at Drumcondra
on the outskirts of Dublin and the village of Swords. In 1773
the coach from Drogheda was held up at Santry by two polite
and well-dressed young men who helped themselves to the cash,
watches and valuables of the travellers. Noticing that one of the
passengers was a priest, they handed back his purse with a bow
and a courteous remark. In 1798 a band, calling themselves the
'Innocents' took over £300 from the north-bound coach, as well
as the weapons of the guard and passengers. Again in the same
year the coach was stopped near the same place and the occupants
were escorted to a nearby house while the coach was heaped with
dry furze and set on fire. On this occasion there was no robbery,
and it appears to have been the work of a party of insurgents who
wished to destroy the mails. Early in the nineteenth century the
notorious Collier stopped the coach from Dublin to Belfast on
the same road and took everything of value from the passengers.
He did this single-handedly. The road was slippery with snow
and the coach was crawling along, and the bold Collier had made
several dummies out of old clothes and straw which he arranged

on the fences holding sticks like muskets. This show of force was enough to frighten the guards, who laid down the blunderbusses. Having plundered them, Collier waved them on with every good wish for a pleasant journey. In 1829 another robber tried his hand at the same game, but was shot dead, and was buried in Santry churchyard. Another attempt on the same road misfired because the occupant of the outside car was a fiery gentleman on his way home from a day's shooting with a couple of loaded fowling pieces on the seat beside him, and, since a robber is an easy mark for a man accustomed to bringing down snipe on the wing, he shot one of them dead and severely wounded a second the moment he saw their intention. The others ran for their lives, and he was sportsman enough to bring the wounded man to a doctor.

An old proverb says that a poor man can dance before a robber, but, unfortunately, this is not always the case. The robbers waiting for a rich prize at Drumcondra bridge one November night in 1768 were so enraged when their first victim had no money that they threw him over the bridge into the Tolka river. Another horrible affair occurred in June 1807 when a good priest, Fr MacCartan, was walking home from the house of a friend near Lucan. He was shot down without warning by a group of robbers who then relieved him of all that he possessed – a cheap silver watch and ten shillings. Shortly afterwards the robbers were captured; one of them informed on the others and they were hanged. Lord Charlemont was held up and robbed near his house at Marino no less than three times – the poor man must have been an easy mark for thieves.

In March 1799 the Limerick Mail was stopped near Maryborough by thirteen men and everything was taken from the passengers, as well as all the mails. In 1808 the Protestant bishop of Limerick, travelling out from the city with a few friends, was held up and his coach rifled, although the occupants made some resistance, the bishop himself being wounded in the struggle. In 1811 the Cork Mail was robbed in County Tipperary and in 1812 the Derry coach was held up near Collon in County Louth.

Travelling certainly was an adventure in those days. Not all the holding up of coaches was for the sake of robbery. Often it was the work of insurgent bands whose only purpose was to take the arms of the passengers and guards, or to destroy documents which were dangerous to them in the mails. Often, too, the assailants were Whiteboys looking for tithe proctors or landlords' minions, who might be severely mishandled. A favourite punishment for these officials, who were regarded as public enemies by the common people, was being forced to kneel down on the road and to eat their warrants or writs of eviction; the more humane Whiteboys would allow them a drink of water, or even a mug of beer to wash the paper down.

But the one who caught the imagination of the public was the romantic highwayman on horseback with his mask and pistols who robbed the rich and helped the poor in good old style. There were many of these. Some of them were gentlemen driven from their lands by the confiscations of Cromwell and Dutch William. Redmond O'Hanlon was the hero of the poor people and the terror of the rich landlords in Armagh and the neighbouring counties for nearly twenty years. O'Hanlon collected a band of desperate men, outlawed by the confiscations like himself and proclaimed that he had appointed himself Chief Ranger of the Mountains, Surveyor General of the High Roads, Lord Examiner of All Travellers and High Protector of his Benefactors and Contributors. A reward of £400 – a mighty sum in those days – was put on his head, and £40 each of his men, and although many of the country people knew of his haunts, none of them would touch the blood money. On one occasion the authorities offered him pardon and riches if he would join in the scheme to bring false charges of a 'Popish Plot' against Oliver Plunkett, the saintly archbishop of Armagh, but the gallant Redmond spurned the offer. Many of his adventures are still told in his native county, and curses are still heaped upon his foster-brother Art O'Hanlon who, although his trusted friend, murdered him for the reward. His head was taken and stuck on a spike over the gate of Downpatrick jail.

Another tragic victim of the wars was Eamonn a' Chnoic, Edmund Ryan of Atshanboe in County Tipperary, who fought at the Boyne and Aughrim, and was forced into outlawry. His kindness to the poor and his preying upon the rich are the basis of many a tale. Until one night he took refuge in the house of a farmer whom he believed to be friendly, but who hungered for the reward and struck him down with a hatchet and cut off his head. The murderer was disappointed in his plan, however, for on arriving at Clonmel with the head he was blandly informed that a pardon had been issued and no reward was forthcoming.

Up on the Comeraghs between Carrick-on-Suir and Dungarvan they still point out Crotty's Rock, a high spike from which the robber watched the country around. Crotty was no patriot; he robbed for money. But he was generous to the poor and they often helped him in daring escapes. He knew every inch of the countryside and could run like a hare. His den in a deep cave near the Rock, so difficult to get into that he was cornered in it a number of times but always escaped. His wife used to keep watch from the rock while he snatched a few hours' sleep in the cave, but a false friend enticed him to stay at his house and, having plied him with spirits until he was hopelessly drunk, sent for the soldiers and Crotty was hanged outside Waterford. His wife was hunted as an accomplice, but when the pursuit was near she jumped off the rock and was killed on the stones below.

Another merry rogue was Charles O'Dempsey of Laois, known as 'Cathair na gCapall' because of his skill at stealing and coping horses. It is said that he could steal a horse, disguise it and sell it back to its former owner, and that he went so far as to take apprentices and teach them his nefarious trade. At one stage he tried to get a local landlord condemned for stealing some horses which he himself had hidden on the landlord's property, even swearing against him in the court. The landlord was acquitted but was so enraged that he hunted out proof against Cathair and saw him hanged in Maryborough in the year 1753.

Few of the highwaymen escaped the penalty of the law. The famous Freeny, who operated mainly in County Kilkenny, cheated the gallows in the end. Many of his associates were taken and hanged but Freeny himself in some way gained the influence of Lord Carrick and was pardoned. Incidentally the authorities thought that his special talents should not be wasted, and gave him a job as customs man and water-bailiff in New Ross, in which comparatively peaceful occupation he ended his days. Collier was another who escaped. His exploits along the borders of Dublin and Meath were many and daring. Once he broke out of Trim jail and swam across the Boyne in a hail of musket-balls and on another occasion he was almost at his last gasp being chased by a patrol when some friendly potato-diggers hid him in a heap of potatoes. At length he was caught and transported to Australia, but some years later he turned up again in County Meath and settled down quietly in Navan. The neighbours could not tell how he lived, but years afterwards it was revealed that he had turned a common informer and that his income was provided by the authorities in return for his spying on the Young Irelanders.

William Brennan – known in song as 'Brennan on the Moor' – worked the roads from Clonmel to Killarney, and more than once held up and robbed the very soldiers sent out to capture him. The song tells us that he was captured and hanged in Clonmel, but another version of his death is that he tried to hold up and rob a Kerry lawyer named Jeremiah O'Connor on the road from Millstreet to Killarney. Brennan levelled his blunderbuss at O'Connor and demanded his purse. O'Connor held out the purse in his left hand and at the same time whipped out a pistol and shot Brennan dead.

Richard Power of Kilbolane had the merry habit of waiting until the rents were collected and the receipts safely in the hands of the tenants. Then he held up the landlord's agent and halved the loot with the tenants. On the occasion of a wedding in Newcastle West, Power turned up among the guests and drank to the health of the bride and then forced the bride's father to hand over his daughter's dowry. He visited the north of Ireland and there tried to hold up a wayfarer at sword point, but the intended victim was not daunted and a brisk duel followed, until the other revealed himself as Redmond O'Hanlon and the two swore friendship. Some time later O'Hanlon saved Power from the gallows by liberally dosing the soldiers on guard with whiskey, so that his friend could escape. Power was betrayed by his sweetheart, who poured water into his pistols while he was asleep and then sent for the soldiers, and, as the song says 'he couldn't shoot the water and a prisoner he was taken'. He was hanged in public at Clonmel in 1685.

Few of them escaped the law. Paul Liddy escaped twice from jail, but in the end took poison on the night before he was due to be hanged. Charles Carraher, a dreadful scoundrel who haunted the roads north of Dundalk, was hanged on the roadside where he was taken in the very act of robbing a passer-by, and few mourned him because of his cruelty. Jeremiah Grant, made famous by George Borrow, had five years of robbery to his credit when he died on the gallows in Maryborough in 1816. Still less fortunate was William Delaney of Upperwood, who was hanged in Naas, and by an error of the executioner cut down too soon and revived by his friends, only to be taken again in Kilkenny for petty robbery and hanged by a more expert practitioner. They had a gay time while it lasted, cutting fine figures and spending guineas like water, but the law had the last word.

❖ SPREADING THE NEWS

One night, in the local, the talk turned to radio, television and allied subject, and one, more honest than the rest, admitted that he knew nothing about it. The know-all of the parish began to put him right as follows:

> "Tis how you don't understand radio? I suppose you don't know how the telephone works either? Well, do you see that dog there? If you stood on his tail, wouldn't he yelp at the other end? And if he was a dog five miles long, wouldn't he yelp five miles away from you, and you standing on his tail? Well, that's just how the telephone works.' (Pause) 'Oh, the radio? Sure 'tis the very exact same, only you haven't any dog there.'

The reaction of the recipient of this lecture on modern communication systems is not fully recorded, and perhaps it is best so. Such explanations are part of the hazard of modern life; our great-great-grandfathers, quietly sitting in little thatched pubs, sipping porter from pewter mugs might discuss the vote for the forty-shilling freeholder at their ease, uninterrupted by technical quibbles of the sort that plague us now. For the telegraph is little over a hundred years old, the telephone is from our grandfathers' day, the radio from our fathers' time, and we ourselves have seen the coming of the television. What form of communication will be used by our children we can guess at – maybe some form of portable dial two-way radio with a television-window, small enough to be carried in the pocket, on which they can see and speak to friends at any time. Models may be made to go on the wrist like a watch; indeed the wristwatch will not be needed any longer when we can dial the central observatory and see the exact time, Greenwich mean, solar or what you will.

It is a strange fact, and one very hard for us to understand, that some people have the gift of mental communication. We have all heard of second sight, and some of us may have personal experience of it, but second sight – the gift of knowing what is happening at some distant place – apparently comes unexpectedly and cannot be called up at will. There are people whom we, bogged down as we are in a morass of all sorts of gadgets, would call savages who have this faculty of telepathy. In the remote deserts of Australia among the 'Wild Blacks', who live in a very simple way by collecting whatever food they can find, this gift is said to be quite common. An old man can sit down and go into a sort of a trance and think thoughts into the heads of people a hundred miles away. It often happens that a cowboy or a shepherd announces to his boss that he must go home to his tribe, someone is dead or some important meeting is to be held, but, don't worry, he'll be back again as soon as the business is over. How does he know that he is wanted? He knows that he knows but how to explain it to those who seem to be so clever in so many ways but are like small children when it comes to sending thoughts over a distance? Some American Indian tribes had the same gift, especially on the prairies; in fact it seems to belong to very simple nomadic people who live in very wide, open empty spaces.

Our own remote ancestors do not seem to have had this gift. But then, when history begins for us about eighteen hundred years ago, they already had a high degree of culture, a complicated social system and an advanced knowledge of the arts and crafts of the time – all very much nearer to us and our way of life than are the nomadic Indians or Australians of the twentieth century. If they wanted to communicate over a distance, they had to do it as our own great-great-grandfathers would have done it a hundred and fifty years ago, by sounds, by signs or by sending a messenger. We are told of loud-voiced men whose shout, like that of a sergeant-major, could be heard above the din of battle, but the distance to which even their voices carried was limited. Horns or trumpets were used to give signals as well as to produce music, and there are splendid specimens of trumpets of cast bronze in the National Museum; some of these produce sweet musical notes and appear to be musical instruments, but others give out a bellowing roar and must be signal trumpets. We know that trumpets were used in battle not only to frighten and overawe the enemy by their sound but also to make different calls or notes as signals 'for battle, for unyoking or for marching, for sleep or for council' as an army bugler does today. And even though a fine bronze trumpet might be a bit on the expensive side for a fisherman or a farmer to own, there always were cow and sheep horns which can so easily be made into signal trumpets and used to convey simple signals, to call the men home from the fields or to signal from boat to boat. Such horns were still in use in parts of Ireland during the last century, and it is related that they were used to call people to Mass when the Penal Laws were being relaxed but bells had not yet come back to the little Catholic chapels of the time. Similar horns – some of them made by cutting the bottoms off pint bottles – were sounded in 1920–21 to tell of the approach of Black and Tan lorries.

Visible signs have been made as long as the need for signals has existed, that is from the very remotest times. A flag or a cloth waved in the air or displayed on a prominent place is quite an obvious signal, and signs could be prearranged so that an onlooker not 'in the know' remained ignorant of the meaning and even unaware that it was a signal. A woman coming out of a kitchen door and shaking a sheet or a tablecloth as if to dust it, or a sheet spread on a certain bush or on the thatched roof 'to dry' could and often did mean that it was safe to approach the house or that the Yeomen were on the move, and the scouts up on the hills acted accordingly. Beacon fires giving a volume of smoke by day or a bright light by night were commonly used to indicate danger or rejoicing. When Daniel O'Connell won the Clare election bonfires were lit on many of the hills of County Clare, and watchers in Galway, Limerick and Tipperary were waiting beside their piles of turf and bogdeal on the hills to send the good news farther. And it is probable that the customary bonfires on Midsummer Eve or May Eve were originally intended to announce far and wide the coming of the important season.

In ancient Ireland men who carried important messages were known by certain signs. In the *Táin Bó Chuailgne* we read of such a messenger from the enemy host coming to Cúchulainn bearing a white hazel staff in one hand and a naked sword in the other. 'Good, my lad,' said Cúchulainn, 'these are the tokens of a herald' to a youth of his following who did not recognise the signs which gave the messenger the right of uninterrupted passage. In later times Irish couriers were famous for their prowess in running across difficult country where a mounted messenger could not travel, through forests and over bogs and rocks. A very good drawing by an Englishman, named Derricke, who served Queen Elizabeth in Ireland, was published in the year 1581. It shows the delivery of a letter to the lord deputy, Sir Henry Sidney – the messenger is handing him the letter with the word 'Shogh' – Derricke's spelling of the Irish word '*seo*'! (here, here it is). The messenger is a sturdy bearded man with bare legs and leather shoes, and in his left hand he carries a stout staff which would serve both as a symbol of his office and a jumping staff to help him to clear obstacles in the manner of a pole vaulter.

Of course most messengers were mounted. We know that there were good roads in ancient Ireland, and that rules and regulations for their maintenance are included in the Brehon Laws. In Offaly and Laois in 1600 the English soldiers were surprised to find 'the highways and paths so well beaten', and the English chronicler Fynes Moryson lets the cat out of the bag when he explains this and such other signs of prosperity and order as the ground so manured, the fields so orderly fenced, the towns so frequently inhabited' by telling us 'the reason whereof was the queen's forces during these wars never till then came among them'. A Scotsman, William Lithgow, who travelled the Irish roads in 1619 and 1620 has many complaints about them, telling how he foundered six horses in five months of travel, but this was in winter and the country had not yet recovered from

Elizabeth's wars. Dean Swift, in 1729, complained that the roads were deplorable, yet less than twenty years later a gentleman of the Pakenham family who had travelled extensively on the continent came to see his relatives in County Longford and recorded in his journal that the Irish roads, in his opinion, were the best in Europe.

Up to the middle of the eighteenth century there was no public postal service available to all, and letters had to be sent by specially hired messengers or left to the rather uncertain method of passing from one person to another until they reached the right place. The first stagecoach from Dublin to Belfast did not run until 1752, and it took more than thirty years before a regular service ran between these cities; it was not until 1784 that a post office was established in Ireland with a postmaster general to supervise the regular delivery of mails, which hitherto had had to depend upon occasional attention from England. In those days the cost of postage varied according to the distance, and in many places they were carried by private individuals or companies for profit. Sometimes the sender paid the postage and sometimes it was paid by the recipient and some carriers charged both parties. So there was no uniformity until the governmental postal service gradually extended over the country. Mails were still carried by privately owned coach or car lines, such as Bianconi's famous service, until they were gradually taken over by the railways, but the horse-drawn 'post car' is still remembered, by many not so old people, as the immediate predecessor of the modern motor-van. Finally, in 1840, the plan of the progressive Sir Rowland Hill was put into operation, all the more remarkably as Hill was not an official of the post office. His plan was, as we know, the penny post, by which a small letter could be sent for one penny to any point in Great Britain or Ireland, and the first adhesive postage stamp, the famous 'penny black', covered the cost of postage. Hill's reforms were adopted or adapted in other places and the various countries of the world by degrees linked themselves together into a general postal union to ensure quick and sure delivery to almost any part of the globe.

From time to time we still hear of messages sent in sealed bottles thrown into the sea or by carrier pigeon, but these nowadays are by way of novelty, competition or advertisement. And it may now be revealed that the report circulated during the recent war to the effect that the Department of Defence had succeeded in producing a hybrid of pigeon and parrot which could not only fly swiftly to a given destination but also, on arrival, deliver a verbal message, was not founded strictly on fact but was probably a rumour thought up by some bright intelligence officer and deliberately noised about to cause dismay and confusion among possible enemies.

❖ THE SUMMER PASTURES

Two thousand five hundred years ago the Greek writer, Pytheas, in a description of north-western Europe, which was more remote from him than Siberia is from us, wrote that the people of 'Thule' had the custom of driving their cattle up into the mountains in the summer, and living there with them until the end of autumn, when they drove them down to the homestead again. This is the earliest account of summer pasturing in this part of the world. What 'Thule' was nobody is quite certain. It may have been Ireland but more likely it was Norway. That does not matter, as the custom was well known in many parts of north-western Europe in later times and even up to our own day.

Here in Ireland it attracted the attention of many English visitors. It was known in parts of Britain, but not in the flat south-eastern half of that land from which most of the English officials came to Ireland, and so it seemed very strange to them. The poet Spenser said that the Irish country people 'kept their cattle and lived themselves the most part of the year in boolies pasturing upon the mountains and wild waste plains, removing to fresh land as they had depastured the former', and, like other English writers, Spenser concluded that the Irish lived a nomad life without any really fixed home. A casual observer might easily make that mistake, but the real state of affairs was quite different. It was a matter of simple mathematics, as simple as 'two and two make four'. If you could take away the cattle from the fields around the house all during the summer and autumn, you could have more hay and a bit of winter pasture. Therefore you could keep more cattle and were a richer man. But where could you put the cattle in summer and autumn?

In Ireland, as in other parts of north-western Europe there are big areas of the countryside which have some value during the better part of the year but none at all during the winter and spring. These are, of course, the mountains and moor lands. In the cold season they are barren and desolate, but when the milder part of the year comes they provide grazing which may be sparse but is very sweet. Our farming ancestors knew this even in remote times, and made full use of the knowledge. Nowadays we pasture sheep or dry cattle on them, but these were much less important than milking cattle in former times and a system was worked out which gave the milch-cows the benefit of them. They were away in the mountains or the moors, far from the homestead over bad roads or no roads at all, so that the cattle could not be driven home for milking, or even the milk brought home morning and evening. The answer was quite clear. Some of the family went and lived with the cows on the mountain. Some sort of dwelling was built there for them, they milked the cows morning and evening and made the butter which could be stored until the men from the home farm came for it once a week or so. And this type of farm economy became quite the ordinary thing in any district within reach of a suitable stretch of moorland or mountain. It lasted up to quite recently – there are people still alive in several parts of Ireland who took part in it in their young days.

When the move to the summer pastures was being planned, the first thing done was the preparation of the houses or huts in which those in charge of the cattle would live. After the harsh wind and rain of the winter they would need repairing, and often the old ones had to be rebuilt or entirely new ones built. Different kinds were used in different places, and the remains of many of them are still to be seen. Most of them were just rough copies of the kind of houses ordinarily used as dwellings, smaller and simpler but made of the same materials and by the same methods. Usually they had only one room, with a simple fireplace, often without any chimney, only a hole in the roof over the hearth. Of course they were occupied only in the summer and autumn, in fine weather when their occupants could live out of doors all through the long period of daylight, coming in only to sleep or to cook food and eat it. Indeed the cooking and eating was often done in the open, too, and the *buaile* houses were used as sleeping-places only, except in rainy weather.

But there were some rather unusual types of structure also. In some places, Donegal, for instance, or north-west Mayo or parts of the Bog of Allen, the *buaile* houses were partly underground, usually dug into a sloping bank of sandy or gravelly soil. These huts were about eighteen feet long and ten feet wide. The site was chosen with some care on a slope which faced the good weather-point, usually south. A party of men went up to prepare the site and build the hut; they dug away at the slope until they had a large enough space; they usually chose a slope of forty-five degrees or so, which meant that the cut-away part of the slope was high enough to form the back wall of the hut, which needed only a front wall and part of the side walls built of stones or sods or whatever material came easiest to hand. Spaces for a door and a window or two were left in the front wall and a rough hearth was made at one end. The whole hut was covered with a strong roof, and often the timber for this could be found – in the form of bog-deal or bog-oak – close at hand; the roof was sodded and thatched in the ordinary way. The furniture was of the simplest kind. A good thickness of heather and dry grass, covered with blankets, made the beds. A few stools or straw 'bosses' to sit on, and even these might be made from materials close to hand, bundles of heather or chunks of bog-wood. A chest or two to keep food and clothing in, a few cooking utensils and a pot hanger. All rather rough, perhaps, but clean and dry and comfortable. The site was usually in a little mountain valley, close to a stream, the kind of a place you would select for a picnic or a hikers' camp.

A traveller in the western part of County Galway in the year 1699 spent some days in a *buaile* house which was built of wicker hurdles plastered with clay:

The house was one entire long roome without any partition. In the middle of it was the fire place with a large wood fire which was no way unpleasing tho in summertime. It had no chimney but a vent hole for

the smoake at the ridge. We all lay in the same roome upon green
rushes. I had sheets and soft white blankets, and they assur'd me no
man ever gott cold by lyeing on green rushes, which indeed are sweet
and cleane, being changed everie day if raine hinders not.

Many a camper of today fares worse than that.

Up on the southern slopes of the Galtees the *buaile* houses
were small rough copies of the dwelling houses down below.
Preparations were made about the middle of April, and the cattle
went up just before May Day and stayed on the mountain pastures
until the end of October. An old 'residenter' who died a few years
ago – Mr Michael Cunningham – gave a description of how things
were done when he was a young lad, that is, about 1875:

> The reason for going up at all was that there was no rent on the
> mountain and the land on the farm below was nearly all put under
> hay to feed the cows in the wintertime. In that way a farmer could
> have a lot more cattle on a small farm. Some of the family used spend
> the whole summer above with the cattle. Sometimes it was the young
> ones that went up and sometimes it was the old people if there was
> a lot of work to be done below and they wanted the young people
> there to do it. They would live in the houses on the mountain all
> summer and only come down to Mass or when they were bringing
> the butter. About from twenty to forty cattle each one would have
> on the mountain. The houses were by themselves with a mile or more
> between them. So that it was kind of lonely sometimes up there, but
> other times they would come together and have a dance or some other
> fun like that.

> The work they did was to milk the cattle night and morning and
> make the butter. When enough of it was made they brought it down
> to the road to be carried to the town [Mitchelstown]. They would
> bring it down the mountain in firkins the cooper used to make, for in
> those days the cooper was an important tradesman in the district, and
> he got plenty to do. Potatoes and buttermilk they used to eat mostly,
> and they had the fresh milk and the butter and oatenmeal bread, and,
> I hear, an odd drop of poitín.

There are traditions about the summer pastures in the Kerry mountains and on the Knockmealdowns, around Slieve Callan in County Clare and on the Blackstairs, on the Wicklow Mountains and the Mournes and the Sperrins, in Donegal and Galway and Leitrim and Mayo. In Achill some people had a number of mountain pastures, with huts on all of them. First the cattle went to one of them, and in a couple of months, when that was grazed out, they moved on to the next, and so on until they had made the most of the pasture.

In many places tradition tells us that sending the cattle to the summer pasture on the mountain was very beneficial to their health, and that cattle affected by certain diseases improved quickly on the mountain. Needless to say, the human occupants of the *buaile* also reaped a benefit of improved health, with open air, good food and plenty of exercise. For the most part it appears that the people who went to the *buaile* were young girls in their late teens or early twenties, often two or three sisters together. They took dogs to protect themselves and the cattle – a couple of hundred years ago there were still wolves in Ireland; the dogs were, of course, trained to help with the herding. And old people tell of the *buaile* as a very happy place, full of song and laughter. On Sunday evenings the girls from several *buailes* would come together and the young men came up from the farms to be with them, and there was music and dancing and gaiety on hillsides that now hear only the bleat of the sheep and the cry of the grouse and the curlew.

Over the last hundred years this form of farm economy has come to an end in Ireland. Changes in population, different methods of making and marketing butter, reclamation of moor and mountain land, better roads and a more important place for sheep and dry cattle all have helped to bring about the change. It is gradually dying out in the other countries, too, although it is still practised in Norway and Sweden and in the Alps and the Pyrenees, where there are very extensive summer grazing grounds and where the custom is likely to survive for a long time yet.

❖ Pistols for Two

Single combat as a method of settling a quarrel is as old as the hills. You find it in all sorts of places, times and circumstances, from the Zulu chieftain spearing his rival to the pair of tinkers squaring up to each other at the fair of Knocknagree. Our old traditional tales are full of it, one of the stock characters being the hero who appears at the gate of the castle to challenge the giant or the tyrant, and, naturally, to defeat him and cut off his head. Dermot Ó Duibhne stands at the ford by the Palace of the Quicken Trees and slays, one after another, the warriors sent to take Fionn and his bewitched comrades; Cúchulainn kills his son Connla and his friend Ferdia in single fight; Oscar the mighty champion defeats all comers and is beaten by none.

In time of war, too, there were single combats. The champion of one army would step forth, before battle was joined, and challenge the champion of the other side, and both armies looked on while the chosen pair fought it out. Sometimes the result of the fight was taken as an omen of victory or defeat and the whole army encouraged or cast down by the success or fate of their hero. Many rulers and famous men had their own champions, who would take their place if they were challenged to combat. Napoleon, who hated duelling and did much to suppress it, ridiculed this system when, on the occasion of his being challenged by the king of Sweden, he announced that he would appoint a famous teacher of swordsmanship as his ambassador to deal with the matter.

A strange form of single combat was the judicial fight or 'wager of battle'. This was common in the middle ages in many countries when disputes between individuals were brought before the courts and the judges could not see clearly where the right and justice lay. Why not leave it to the will of God, they said, and let the plaintiff and the defendant fight it out in presence of the court? The court decided what weapons were to be used – usually only a cudgel or staff and a shield, and the results were not fatal. The result of the fight was taken as God's judgement on the case, and the looser, if he had been accused of a crime, punished in the same way as if his guilt had been proved by evidence and witnesses. The last recorded case of such a trial by combat in Ireland took place in the year 1583 between two gentlemen of the Leinster O'Connors who were persuaded to lay complaints against each other before the Lords Justice in Dublin, and these ordered a trial by combat which was duly held in the courtyard of Dublin castle before a large gathering of spectators. The two disputants, Tadhg and Cormac O'Connor, appeared stripped to their shirts, each armed with a sword, a shield and a helmet, and were searched for hidden weapons and seated on stools at opposite corners of the yard. At the sound of the trumpet they began to fight 'with great valour and resolution'. After a stirring bout Tadhg felled Cormac and 'pommelling him about the head with the hilt of his sword to astonish him' knocked his helmet off and beheaded him, presenting the head to the Lords Justices on the point of his sword. Sir Geoffrey Fenton, the chief secretary, who arranged the combat, had as little interest in the rights and wrongs of the affair as the Lords Justices themselves, for he wrote after the fight 'I would her Majesty had the same end of all the O'Connors in Ireland; then might it be hoped for, that no such disturbance would rise again in Leinster as hath done through their quarrels', and a few days later they tried to stage another fight between two other O'Connors, but one of these claimed that the other was of too low birth to engage in combat and did not turn up for the contest, thus cheating the authorities out of another day's sport and the easy disposal of another enemy.

The duel as a way of settling a private quarrel without any reference to the law of the land became very popular in France during the seventeenth century, although both Church and State spoke out against it. Cardinal Richelieu was loud in condemning duels, and had several duellist executed or otherwise punished while King Louis XIV issued no less than eleven edicts against the practice. Nevertheless it flourished. From France it spread to England, and thence to Ireland where it became a fashion, a habit, a craze among the gentry and squireens of the eighteenth and on into the early years of the nineteenth century. Duels were fought for the most trivial causes, often between close friends and relations. As one gentleman of the period put it, at least one duel was considered a necessary part of a young man's education. And we are told that the reputation of being a fire-eating duellist was most useful in making a good marriage settlement, both in the esteem of the young lady and of her family. We hear of crying infants being consoled with the promise of a pair of duelling pistols, and of children being held up to see their fathers take the field.

For some reason or other lawyers were foremost in their devotion to this 'manly sport', often issuing challenges while arguing a case in the courts. At Clonmel assizes in 1775 a committee of lawyers and other gentlemen drew up and issued a set of rules for the regulation of duels; these rules became known as 'The Thirty-Six Commandments' and copies of them were circulated far and wide. Although many of these firebrands were adept at sword-play, pistols were the favourite duelling weapons. Every lawyer, landlord, squireen and 'half-gintleman' had his case of pistols and put in hours of practice to improve his shooting. In England and on the continent the usual fashion was to provide one pair of pistols and give one of these to each duellist. In Ireland, however, each man brought his own pair and stood ready with one in each hand, ready to blaze away with a right and left. Each contestant brought at least one second, and the seconds made the arrangements for the fight, since the 'principals' were not allowed to speak until the fight was over. Leonard MacNally, the man who posed as a United Irishman and secretly betrayed the leaders of the movement, once fought a duel with Lawyer Barrington in Phoenix Park, and had as his seconds the brothers Henry and John Shears and

Bagenal Harvey. On this occasion MacNally escaped death only because his opponent's bullet struck the buckle of his braces, which led a bystander to remark that he never before heard of a rogue *saved* by the gallows. Sometimes the seconds fell out and challenged each other, and in this case they, too, were provided with pistols and took up their stance at right angles to the line of fire of their principals, and all four began to fire on the word of command. Another functionary usually in attendance was a surgeon, complete with a large bag of instruments, plasters and bandages, ready to attend to the wounded, or to certify the dead, as occasion required.

Perhaps the most famous of all Irish duels was that between Daniel O'Connell and J. N. D'Esterre, which did so much to establish O'Connell as a popular hero, but was a very silly affair when all is said and done. It was fought at Bishopscourt, County Kildare, on 1 February 1815 and, as we know, D'Esterre was severely wounded and died of internal bleeding two days later. The affair was misrepresented then and later as a Catholic versus Protestant affair, but there was no truth in this, for D'Esterre was a man of liberal views and a supporter of Catholic Emancipation. But he was also hot-tempered and reckless, and the cause of the quarrel was O'Connell's reference, in a speech, to the 'beggarly Corporation of Dublin'. D'Esterre was a member of the corporation and called on O'Connell to apologise for the remark. O'Connell refused, and so they fought. Many of O'Connell's supporters in the quarrel, including his second, Major Macnamara, were Protestants, and, before the duel D'Esterre declared that the quarrel had nothing to do with religion. O'Connell was filled with remorse at D'Esterre's death, and also because, as a Catholic, he was forbidden by a decree of the Church to take any part in a duel. It is related that ever afterwards he wore a black glove on his right hand – the hand that shot D'Esterre – whenever he entered a church. Shortly afterwards, on hearing that D'Esterre's widow was engaged in a lawsuit, he threw up all his other legal business in order to plead her case in the courts, and obtained a verdict on her behalf. D'Esterre had the reputation of being a deadly marksman with a pistol, and was a man of proven courage – once, while serving as an officer in the British navy, he was seized by mutineers and threatened with hanging if he did not join them, and, with the rope around his neck, abused them soundly, ending with the shout 'Now, hang away, and be damned to you!', on which the mutineers released him in admiration of his bravery. No wonder the populace, who, by the way, had assembled in large numbers to see the duel, made O'Connell a hero.

A curious form of the duel was known in Ireland in the earlier eighteenth century. The opponents, mounted on horseback, charged each other, firing off a brace of pistols, and if neither was shot they drew their swords and came closer to one another. A famous duel of this kind was fought at Maryborough in 1759 between a Colonel Barrington of Cullenaghmore and a Mr Gilbert. The gallant colonel, when they came to close quarters, stabbed Gilbert's horse and brought it down, then dismounted and forced Gilbert – who was pinned under the horse – to surrender at dagger point, which he did, but only on condition that they should be friends. This duel was attended by great crowds, with mounted men to keep the course clear, and a trumpeter to sound the charge. Another duel in the same town drew a large crowd in 1783. A certain Mr Skelton fell asleep at the dinner table and snored and a certain Mr Roberts, affronted at this, poked the butt end of his whip into Skelton's open mouth and down his throat. Next day they fought on Maryborough Green, and Skelton began the fun by firing off both his pistols and then running for his life. His angry friends dragged him back to stand Roberts' fire, only to find that Roberts had been shot in the leg and could not stand. They argued the case, and decided that Roberts should be tied to a tree to hold him up, so that he could shoot at Skelton. Finally they were persuaded to postpone action, and repaired to the taverns of the town. Roberts now issued a challenge, and Skelton announced that his choice of weapons was his fists, whereupon Roberts, a slight, small man, withdrew, having no chance against the burly Skelton. Many men were wounded, or even lost their lives, in duels just as foolish and trivial.

But there were other meetings inspired by fierce anger or hate, as when two Limerick gentlemen, Massey and White, recognised a poor wretch who had been hanged, as one of their own tradesmen. This poor fellow, a tailor from Rathkeale, had come to dun another landlord for a bill for clothes, and he – perhaps in a drunken frenzy – ordered his men to take the poor tailor and hang him. The friends, in a rage, burst into the tyrant's house and slapped him across the face in the presence of his guests. Then he had to fight. He met Massey on his own front lawn, and Massey, a dead shot, killed him outright at the first discharge of the pistols.

For well over a hundred years the duel flourished among the Irish gentry. The law forbade it and threatened penalties, but the law was here set aside. In eighteenth-century Ireland, the law was the lawyers, the magistrates and the gentry, and the lawyers, the magistrates and the gentry were the foremost duellists. To them the law was no more than an instrument to be used in their own interests and so they twisted it into many queer shapes. Duelling was only one of many signs of their lack of responsibility. Duelling left some of them dead and not a few crippled but their irresponsibility in other things put an end to them as a class.

❖ CAPTAIN MOONLIGHT

My grandmother told me that, when she was a young girl, they were getting up one morning when they heard the most frightful yelling and screaming outside in the fields and when they ran out to see what was wrong they found a man buried up to his neck in the ground, and an old sow that had just been let out by the servant boy eating off one of his ears. They dug him up and bandaged him. He was a rent warner who was a bit too active around the district, but after this he took up some safer job in another part of the country.

Thus an old friend told me a memory of a hundred and fifty years ago, heard from his grandmother, a memory of the Whiteboys and their grim deeds – deeds which brought terror to many and good to very few, deeds which kept the country in an uproar for the best part of a century, and the last echoes of which have scarcely died away in our own time. There is a touch of comedy about the landlord's wretched henchman buried to his neck with a sow breakfasting on his ear, or about that other landlord's man who was travelling by coach and was held up by the Whiteboys and forced to eat his writs of eviction, but provided with a piggin of buttermilk to wash them down. But such humorous asides were few and far between. For the most part the note was that of tragedy.

It all seems to have begun in 1760 when one William Fant of Fantstown, near Kilmallock, a lawyer and gentleman farmer, became deranged in his mind and decided to settle certain grievances against the landed gentry of the neighbourhood in his own way. On a marketday in the town he gathered a large crowd around him and made a violent speech, alleging that certain lands were commons illegally enclosed, and then led the crowd to demolish the fences. The idea became popular and similar bands began to operate in several parts of Munster and beyond. From levelling fences they went on to maiming cattle, burning hay, trampling growing crops, and finally attacking and abusing people, setting fire to houses and killing men, women and children.

It was not just a case of persecuted tenants rising against cruel landlords, although many a landlord, agent and bailiff moderated his demands at the thought of the men in white. Sometimes it was tenant against landlord, but just as often it was cottier and labourer against farmer or small farmer against big farmer. Sometimes it was labourer against labourer, when men combined to deny work to men from other districts or even to men from their own district whose claim, they held, was not as great as their own. They were known by many names, Steelboys, Levellers, Oakboys, Rockites, Molly Maguires, in different parts of the country, but their methods were much the same everywhere. They assembled at night, in disguise, sometimes on horseback, sometimes afoot, to carry out their raids. One disguise was very popular; it was already well-known in more innocent activities, as it was worn by the Biddy boys on St Brighid's Eve and by the Strawboys at country weddings. It consisted of a woman's skirt and a white shirt worn outside the clothes and a cowl or mask of straw over the head. This disguised the figure as well as the face. Some of them blackened their faces with soot instead of wearing a mask; with or without the mask their aspect was terrifying, and often it needed only their appearance outside a man's house to have him instantly yield to their demands, heavy though these might be – that he should leave his farm, that he should refuse to pay rent and so risk eviction, that he should dismiss such and such a workman and employ this other one instead. The white shirts became a symbol of violence and gave them their most popular name, the Whiteboys.

One of their activities was raiding for arms. It was in such a raid that Major Hare of Coolcappa in County Limerick was killed. The raiders crept in through a window and were moving up the stairs when the major heard a noise and rushed out on the landing in his nightshirt with a pistol in his hand, only to be shot down – some still say by accident. He died in his wife's arms, while the raiders made off with his pistols and fowling piece. Another raid, also near Rathkeale, had a sad sequel; the raiders had taken the shotgun of an elderly farmer named Sparling, and beaten him into the bargain. Four men were arrested, tried, condemned and hanged in public on the fair green of Adare, although it was quite clear from the evidence that they were all innocent. Another tale of the hanging of innocent men comes from the west of County Limerick, where two men were brought from Kerry and hanged at Sinan's gate on the Glin road out from Athea. Before they were strung up one of them begged the soldiers to untie his hands a moment, and then took off his good frieze coat and his shoes, a new pair, and gave them to his son who was in the assembled crowd. 'Maybe 'twas how,' said the old people, 'the poor man had nothing else to leave his son, and if he was hanged in them he'd be buried in them. But 'tis said that they were innocent of the crime they were hanged for. No matter, for in those days someone had to be hanged for every crime, and if they couldn't catch the guilty one, well, they hanged an innocent one to frighten the people.' This last statement is only too often true. Human life – at least that of the poor – was little considered in those days, and there were dozens of crimes for which sentence of death was passed. In east Limerick the tale is still told of how the tyrant Ormsby was discoursing to his guests one day on his power and influence, to illustrate which he ordered his servants to seize a poor tramp who was passing on the road and hang him then and there, which they did. The landlords made their own laws; they were the magistrates and lawyers, and if at any time their power and privileges were threatened, they spared no poor man in their determination to uphold their position. They had no mercy on the Whiteboys, although some of them did not hesitate to encourage the Whiteboys against their own enemies, as did Fant of Fantstown.

One Sunday afternoon, in July 1786, a large number of people gathered in a field near Ardagh for sports and other jollifications, but the gathering was mistaken by a jittery cavalry officer named Scalan for a Whiteboy meeting, and he ordered his men to fire, killing six people, and wounding nearly forty. A few years later, in 1793, a large and well-armed band invaded the town of Bruff and fought it out with a regiment of soldiers, many being killed on both sides. Prisoners taken on such occasions had little hope of mercy. Even if they escaped the gallows they faced flogging or transportation. Some were sentenced to as many as a thousand lashes, and were dragged around and flogged in several towns, one after the other, and not a few died under this torture like Staker Wallace, the popular hero of Kilfinane.

The Whiteboys were much opposed to the tithes collected by the Established Church. These fell heaviest on the poor, for while pasture land was free of tithe, thus benefiting the wealthy stock raisers and dairy farmers, they were taken from the poor man's oats, potatoes and flax, and the tithe proctors' methods were as far from gentle as the attitude of the clergy who got the tithes was – in too many cases – far from Christian. In August 1822 nearly two hundred Whiteboys surrounded the house of a tithe protector near Askeaton and had the wretched man on his knees, promising to amend his ways, when the military came upon them and a fight began, in which there were losses on both sides. The government force came back to Rathkeale with five prisoners, two of whom were badly wounded. Major Going, who was in charge of the police and military made the unwounded prisoners dig a grave on the riverbank and then had the badly wounded men – one of the two still conscious – thrown in and covered with quicklime. The others were hanged from the bridge and thrown into the grave. Shortly afterwards the comrades of the dead men raided Going's house, bringing bags of lime in which they intended to bury him alive, but he escaped and took refuge in the house of a local landlord, and when his pursuers arrived there and searched the house, he hid inside a grandfather-clock and so escaped. But some weeks afterwards he was shot on the roadside east of Rathkeale. Three men were arrested for this, of whom two were hanged, the third turning evidence against them. It is said that the informer, ever afterwards while he lived, slept with his eyes open.

It must not be thought, because of their campaign against the tithes, that the Whiteboys were devoted champions of religion. Far from it. In places they went so far as to publish scales of remuneration of priests and clergymen of all denominations for their services, and more than one priest fell a victim to them. In 1819 a certain Fr John Mulqueen was acting as parish priest of Bulgaden while the old pastor was incapacitated through age and illness. Fr Mulqueen was a popular man, noted for his good works and kindness. One night in that year he was returning on horseback from a sick call when he came upon a group of armed Whiteboys, and proceeded to read them a lecture on their evil ways, when one of them raised his gun and shot the priest dead. Rich and poor, Protestant and Catholic subscribed to a fund which provided a reward of £500 for the murderers, but they were never captured. Nearly twenty years before that another parish priest was the victim of a raiding band. This was in Abbeyfeale, shortly after Christmas when Fr David O'Sullivan was assaulted in his own house and tortured to make him reveal the whereabouts of the Christmas offerings paid to him by his flock; the unfortunate clergyman was put sitting on the kitchen fire and was severely burned, but refused to give them any information until they had to run off when help came. Some blamed the Whiteboys for this outrage, but others held that it was a band of common robbers. At least one priest took active measures against the Whiteboys, when, on Easter Monday 1822, word was brought to Fr Rochford, just as he finished Mass in Rathcahill, that a masked band had assembled to burn a house in the neighbourhood. He called on his flock to arm themselves and led them to the rescue. The attackers showed fight, but a party of young gentlemen from Newcastle West, who were fowling on the hills nearby, joined in on the side of the parishioners and drove off the raiders, capturing eight of them, including their leader who was revealed as a whiskey distiller from

Limerick city, while the other prisoners were from respectable families in other parts of the county. The whole thing was revealed as a drunken prank, but shots had been fired and a dwelling-house burned, and so the prisoners were tried, convicted and sentenced to transportation.

Most famous of all the Limerick Whiteboys was one Walter Fitzmaurice, a blacksmith who kept a forge at the foot of Bearna hill, west of Newcastle, and who, under the name 'Captain Rock', set himself up as a champion of the poor and the oppressed. However, in the end his chief exploits were the murder of a youth named Hoskins, whose only crime was that his father was a landlord's agent, and the kidnapping of a young woman named Gould, who was reputed to be a rich heiress, in order to force her to marry his friend, John Browne. This last outrage roused the law and Fitzmaurice and several of his men were named as the perpetrators. In the end several were captured, and others, including 'Captain Rock' himself, surrendered, and although a number of them were hanged and others transported, the two leaders, Fitzmaurice and one Dillane who had fired the shot that killed young Hoskins, were freed, Dillane because he informed on his comrades and 'Rock', although sentenced to death, reprieved through the influence of friends.

The last word on the Whiteboys may be left to Sir George Lewis, one of the commissioners appointed to enquire into the condition of the poorer people in Ireland, 'If every labourer in Ireland could earn eightpence a day for 310 days in the year we should probably never hear of Whiteboy disturbances.' Poverty and oppression breed strange ills, and Ireland was not alone in its troubles; indeed the Whiteboys and their doings look insignificant in comparison with the uprisings and disturbances which shook other countries in Europe at the time.

❖ THE FOOT OF THE RAINBOW

Word went around the parish like wildfire. 'Levelling the old chimney in Seana-Mhuiris' *bothán* is what Mickeen was doing when the pickaxe hopped off an old canister, and if there was one sovereign in it there was fifty!' in actual fact, poor Mickeen had no such luck; there were six sovereigns and a few half-crowns in the mustard tin he found. And by the time he had stood to all his wellwishers he had a hole in his week's wages as well as having said goodbye to his golden fortune. But was he believed? People are still wondering what he did with all his wealth, for by the time the tale had reached the end of the next parish, the fifty was five hundred – 'the full of a three-legged pot, I'm telling you, and it all gold and silver coins!'

The hope of getting something for nothing is, no doubt, part of it, but there is more than this in the fascination which buried treasure holds for every one of us. It may be all the stories we heard as children. Of the crock of gold in the fort, and of the three men who went to dig it and saw their houses burning and had to run off home to save them. And of the cow's skin full of valuables that the monks buried in the field behind the blessed well when they heard that Cromwell's soldiers were coming; that one is guarded by the ghost of a black bull and no one can find it except a monk of the same order. And of the boy who turned a sod and found a treasure and marked the spot with a white stone, but when he returned there were hundreds of white stones in the field and no knowing which was the right one. And of the gold at the foot of the rainbow, which many of us set out to find, with spade on small shoulder, in our innocent childhood.

And, of course, of Paddy Ahern who dreamed three nights one after the other that he'd find a bag of money buried under

Banogue bridge, and walked thirty miles there to look for it. He was poking around above on the bridge and below the bridge until an old man of the place would contain his curiosity no longer. 'Is it any harm to ask what you are doing there, young fellow?' 'Such a thing, sir,' say Paddy, ''Twas a dream I had three nights in a row that there was gold hidden near the bridge.' 'Wisha, you foolish boy, isn't it often I dreamt that there was the world of gold buried under a hawthorn bush in the haggard of one Paddy Ahern away in the west of the county! But sure dreams like that are all foolishness!' 'Well, I suppose they are, sir, and I suppose you're right, sir,' says my brave Paddy, not pretending anything, and away home with him, and there, sure enough, was the gold safely buried in an old crock. A while afterwards, with Paddy in ease and comfort, who should come the way but a poor scholar of great learning, and put up at Paddy's house for the night. 'That's a queer old crock you have,' says the poor scholar. 'And a lucky crock for me,' says Paddy. 'And queer old writing on it in the old Ogham characters,' says the poor scholar. 'Is that writing? 'Twas how I thought it was a sort of an ornament,' says Paddy. 'I'll read it for you,' says the poor scholar, 'although 'tis few could do as much. This is what it says – *Twice as much on the other side*.' 'My brave man,' says Paddy, 'and if that's true for you, you're the lucky man, for I'll halve it with you!' out they went and there was the other crock, twice as big and full to the brim with gold on the other side of the bush. So Paddy became the richest man in the parish, and the poor scholar bought a big house and started the finest school in the country. 'A fine story if it was true,' was the local verdict on this, and well they might doubt, for the same story is told in many counties.

But not all the stories of treasure are false. Precious objects and hoards are found from time to time, and more often than is usually believed. Take County Clare alone, for instance. Only twenty years ago a little girl driving the cows to the fields found a number of silver coins, and when her father dug in the place more than a thousand coins of about AD 1200 came to light. Not twenty years earlier a boy hunting rabbits in north Clare pulled a shining object out of a crevice in the crag, and it was later identified as a 'gorget', a gold collar of nearly two thousand years ago, more than a foot across and over half a pound in weight. Just over a hundred years ago when the railway from Limerick to Ennis was being laid, the workmen engaged in making a cutting came upon the greatest treasure find of recent times. Nobody knows exactly how great it was, for it was quickly divided up – the workmen grabbed up the objects and sold them off as best they could, and, as we may expect, got much less for them than they would have 'through the proper channels'. Certainly there were hundreds of objects there, mostly heavy gold bracelets, and the real value of the find, in today's money, would probably exceed £10,000. Three great finds in one county, and they could be echoed in almost every county. Cross the Shannon from Clare and you hear of the Roman silver found near Foynes or of that finest of all examples of the art of our early Christian ancestors, the Ardagh Chalice found by a workman in the fort at Ardagh. Go north from Clare and you have Galway and the Moylough belt shrine found by a turf cutter during the war; on into County Mayo to hear of the astonishment of the worthy schoolmaster at Balla when one of the boys brought him a large gold 'fibula', a curved bar with a cup-like expansion at each end, something like a huge cufflink, about six inches across. All these, together with many hundreds of other gold and silver treasures, can be seen in the National Museum in Dublin to prove that so many tales of hidden wealth are true.

All very well, says the critic, but why all the noise about treasure that has been found? What about the hidden wealth that hasn't been found yet? A fair objection and a reasonable question. And some of it lies nearer than the foot of the rainbow. Under the gloomy cliffs of Comshingaun in County Waterford, so we are told, is hidden a riding boot full of guineas, stored away against a rainy day by the famous highwayman Crotty, who was betrayed and hanged before he could spend it; the only one who shared his secret was his wife, and she, poor thing, went berserk at the death of her husband and forgot all about the hidden hoard. Not very far away, near Killaughrim in County Wexford another notorious knight of the road hid his ill-gotten wealth and this has not yet been found in spite of long searching. Smugglers, too, had their hoards. A keg of gold is said to be hidden in the depths of a cave which can only be reached by boat between Ballybunion and Beal, and another cave, this one near Clogher in County Louth, has a similar cache.

All along the coasts of Ireland you can hear stories of pirates and wreckers, of lost ships and sunken treasure chests. Take the case of the *Earl of Sandwich* on a voyage from America. This ship was found drifting off the Waterford coast, and when the crew of another ship boarded her they found that her captain, two sailors, two boys and a passenger and his wife and daughter had all been murdered in their sleep and the sea-cocks opened so that the ship would sink. The ship's papers showed that a great sum in silver dollars had been entrusted to the captain and this was missing. Meanwhile four strangers had aroused suspicion in Ballybrasil and New Ross, and soon the hue and cry was on and the men were taken; they were the cook, the boatswain and two seamen from the unlucky ship who had murdered the others and stolen the treasure. Later came soldiers from Duncannon Fort, searching along the shore, and they dug up two hundred and fifty bags of dollars which had been hidden in several different places around what has ever since been called Dollar Bay. The villains were tried in Dublin, executed, and their bodies hanged in chains on the Muglins rocks off Dalkey, but the story goes that not all the treasure was found and that bags of silver dollars still lie around Dollar Bay.

Then there was the Golden Lion, a Danish ship which ran aground in a storm near Kerry Head in the autumn of 1728. The people on board were saved and so was twenty thousand pounds worth of coin and bar silver which was stored at the house of the local landlord, Crosbie. But one dark night, shortly after this the Danish sentries were knocked down and tied up and the silver disappeared. The true facts never came to light and very little of the treasure was ever recovered. Local tradition still maintains that hoards of silver are hidden in the sandhills and along the cliffs.

'Sixty thousand ducats in coined money and as much again in gold and silver plate,' said the only survivor of the ship *Saint Mary of the Rose*, one of the Spanish Armada, which ran on a rock and went down in the Blasket Sound in the month of September 1588. The broken wreck still lies there; about seventy years ago some fishermen tangled their nets on a bronze gun and brought it ashore. Many other ships of the Armada struck on the west coast of Ireland, and each ship had a money chest on board, with gold and silver coin to pay the sailors and soldiers and to buy stores and other necessaries. Few of these money chests were ever recovered. One of them was brought ashore and hidden near Inver Bay in County Mayo, but the fellow who hid it was a half-wit who took the moon for his landmark and, unfortunately, the moon had moved by the time he got back to the treasure. Then there was the *Gran Grin* which went down on the north shore of Clew Bay, the *San Juan of Sicily* and two other ships which broke on Streedagh strand in County Sligo, the *Concepción* which struck near Carna in Connemara, the *Balanzara* sunk near Moville in Inishowen, the *San Marcos* at Spanish Point in County Clare and the *Anunciada* burned and sunk off Carrigaholt in the same county. Some daring frogman may yet make a name and a fortune from one of these.

Inland the tales of treasure are not any less numerous. Pious benefactors in the days of peace gave sacred vessels, rich shrines, bookcovers and vestments to many a church and abbey. Then came the impious freebooters of Queen Elizabeth and Oliver Cromwell, and often the monks or friars were able to hide the holy treasures away before fire and sword ended both their lives and that of their monasteries. We hear of this at Muckross Abbey near Killarney, at Claregalway and Abbeyknockmoy in County Galway, at Mourne Abbey, at Quin, at Holy Cross, at Rattoo, at Mainistir and at scores of other church, abbey and convent ruins. Then there are the castles besieged and taken in the long series of wars. We can be sure that the valuables and money were hidden away during the fight and that some of them were never found, the secret of their hiding-places dying with the slaughtered garrisons. Thus the story runs at Dunboy near Castletownbeare, at Glin and at Carrigogunnel in County Limerick, at Dunamase and Donegal and dozens of others.

Indeed there is hardly an ancient ruin, a burial mound or a stone circle without its story of hidden wealth. There is treasure at the bottom of lakes, guarded by fearsome serpents. There is gold under pillarstones which turn into giants when treasure-hunters come to disturb it. There is the fairy hoard that turns to leaves or ashes in the pocket of the finder. And there still is, and always will be, the crock of gold at the foot of the rainbow.

❖ 'One for Sorrow, Two for Joy'

An unfortunate boy came back to our school after the summer holidays with warts on his hands. In the ordinary way this would have mattered little, and the warts would have yielded to one or other of the numerous traditional cures that we all knew, but the rumour went around that he had plundered a robin's nest, and although he may well have been innocent – as he loudly protested – his life was made a misery for weeks. We all knew the story of how the robin tried to comfort our Saviour on Calvary and was given his red breast as a perpetual memory; the robin must not be hurt or harmed in any way but always treated as a friend, and to our childish minds the robins knew this – hadn't we often seen a robin flying into the kitchen and picking up crumbs from the table? Not that we persecuted other birds, but the robin was sacrosanct. If one got caught in a crib he was released at once with an air of apology; we might keep a linnet or a finch as a song-bird or even try to keep a sparrow as a pet but never a robin. We had heard, too, of another bird at the Crucifixion, the crossbill which tried to draw the thorns from the Saviour's head and was given the crossed bill as a token, but few of us had ever seen this rare bird.

Some people hold that modern farming, with its chemical fertilisers and insecticides has greatly reduced the numbers of wild birds. This may well be true, for it is certain that a small boy's memory of forty years ago is full of birds, and even then the old people held that they were still more numerous in former times. 'Tis many the one would have gone hungry in bad times,' said an elderly neighbour, 'but for the birds they caught. And it wasn't only the big birds but thrushes and blackbirds too. We used to go out in the long nights with a light and dazzle them in the hedges and knock them down with sticks, and 'tis often I saw a dozen or more of them hanging from the crane over the fire, roasting, yes, and 'twas often I ate them too, and I can tell you they tasted nice when you mightn't have seen meat for a month before that.' He told us, too, of his poaching of pheasant and woodcock in the same way, with a lantern and a stick, although the landlords were very severe on poachers, and of setting snares for snipe in marshy places and of sticks smeared with birdlime to catch wood-pigeons in the trees, and even of cormorants that he had seen eaten by fishermen near the mouth of the Shannon, 'but I can tell you they were the strong eating, as tough as an old boot and the taste of every fish the creatures ever ate on them.'

In my day a group of boys might still go 'torching' and persuade their mothers to let them roast a thrush or a blackbird, but the custom was dying out then and is hardly ever heard of now. 'Cribs' are still made sometimes, but only by small boys for amusement, and the captured birds are usually released or kept as pets.

The thrush we respected as a fine singer, and, indeed, the blackbird's musical efforts were praised too, but he was disliked by people who lived in thatched houses as he had the uncomfortable habit of tearing large holes in the thatch, whether to get material for his nest or to search for insects, we were not quite sure. People stuck rods with fluttering rags in the roof to scare the blackbirds or hung up a potato into which a number of feathers had been thrust so that it whirled about in the wind, but the blackbirds became accustomed to these devices in a short while and the holes in the roof appeared again. No wonder that some angry householders made war on the blackbirds or sprinkled salt or soot on the thatch to discourage them. More recently a spraying of bluestone solution on the thatch has proved effective; it is supposed that this discourages insects in the thatch, and the blackbirds have to forage elsewhere. Even the domestic hens were not adverse to poking about in an old thatched roof, and I still remember the loudly expressed joy of an old fellow, who had re-roofed a shed with corrugated iron, at the efforts of his wife's fowl to resume their favourite perch. It took several days of flying up and slithering down again before the silly birds learned that the good old days were gone.

People liked to have rooks about the place. A man with a rookery in his grove of trees was quite proud, and if, by any chance, they deserted the place everybody thought that he must have done something dreadful. A story was told of a tyrant landlord who evicted a poor widow, whereupon all the crows left his estate and did not return until he died. They are knowing birds. They begin to make their nests on 1 March, but if this falls on a Sunday they wait until the next day to begin work. And in the spring, you never see a crow in the bogs until the turf-cutting begins when they come in flocks and you have to hide your dinner-bag away or you'll find they have raided it. The jackdaw, albeit a merry fellow, was looked upon as a bit of a nuisance because of his habit of nesting in chimneys and his impudent thieving ways. The grey-hooded crow, the *córnach* as the old people called him, was hated as a killer of lambs and chickens, and was hunted until he became the wariest of birds. Seldom could we come within a field's distance of a hooded crow.

Housewives disliked the magpie, holding that he stole young chickens, but little or no effort was made to hunt them down, except that a nest too near a fowl-yard might be demolished. We all knew and believed the magpie rhyme –

One for sorrow, two for joy,
Three to get married and four to die,
Five for silver, six for gold,
Seven for a secret never to be told.

– although we were not quite sure what the last line meant. Many people did not feel comfortable at seeing one magpie and looked around to find a second one. I had a pet magpie, found as a fledgling and carefully reared, which used to sit on my shoulder, and there were dire prophecies of ill-luck to come because of the 'one for sorrow'. However, the only ill-luck was for the poor magpie when in his innocence he joined a flock of feeding fowl and was pecked to death by a hatching hen. The magpie is a notable nest builder, and we were told the story of how he tried to teach all the other birds how to make a good nest. 'First,' quoth he, 'you find a suitable branch in a tree.' 'Don't we all know that?' said the crow. 'Then you put two sticks across, like this.' 'That is only common sense,' said the pigeon. 'Then you add more sticks,' continued the magpie patiently. 'We're not learning much here today,' said the blackbird. 'All right,' said the magpie, 'if you know it all, I'm only wasting my time with you.' And the class broke up, never to reassemble. Only the wren watched the master builder in secret, and so only two birds, the magpie and the wren know how to roof a nest.

If you put a pinch of salt on a bird's tail, we were told, the bird cannot fly and you can easily catch it, but if you wanted to catch a heron – we called them 'cranes' – all you had to do was to creep up behind him and shout 'lie down!' in his ear and he would obligingly fall in a faint. But you had to be careful; he always stabbed at your eye when waking up again, and his beak is long and powerful. The water-bailiffs hated herons, accusing them of devouring salmon-spawn, and shot them whenever they could, but we liked to see the great birds, especially if one was flying south as this was a certain sign of good weather. Still a better weather-prophet was the swallow, as she flew high or low to indicate sunshine or rain. Swallows are blessed, said the old people; it is very lucky to have them nesting in the cow-house, and their nests must on no account be harmed even when they are empty – if a swallow's nest in a byre is deliberately harmed the cows in that byre will give blood instead of milk.

Another lucky bird is the cuckoo. 'Thanks be to God and may we live to hear it again,' is what you should say on hearing the cuckoo's first call. Especially lucky it was to hear it in the right ear, not so fortunate to hear it in the left. Many the time I saw an old person, on being told that the cuckoo was calling, turn around so as to be sure to hear it in the right ear. If you heard the cuckoo calling from the trees in the churchyard, that meant a death in the family before the year was out; if you heard it before your breakfast it meant a hungry year for you, and all sorts of unspecified ill-luck fell on the person who was so unfortunate as to hear it from inside the house and not in the open. Another bird whose call held a message was the *cúirliún*, as we called the whimbrel. A single long clear call from him meant fine weather while a quavery repeated call meant rain on the way.

To hear a lot of corncrakes calling in the dusk meant fine weather on the way. There were many arguments as to how the corncrake could produce such a robust noise. Some held that the bird lay on its back when calling, others that it pushed its bill into the ground, and still others that it had no voice at all but made its sound by plucking a wing with a leg – 'the same way as you'd knock a note out of the string of a fiddle'. The noise made by the *gabhairín reó*, the jacksnipe, was also a mystery to us; most people said it was a voice call but others held it was a sound made by the wings. Its call meant frost, and it was usually heard in the cold weather. I liked to lie in the heather and watch its wings quiver as it dived after flies. The green plover was another bird that called the frost.

The old story of the wren betraying St Stephen and the other one of how it warned Cromwell's men of the approach of an Irish force were usually heard around Christmas. In the old days people really hunted the wren on the afternoon of Christmas Day, but that had died out in our time. The wren was not disturbed at other times of the year, and I always thought the story was trotted out at Christmas as a half-hearted excuse for chasing and killing the little creature. But, although we didn't persecute it, we regarded the wren as a sneaky little thing, disliked by all the birds as well as by every other creature since the time it deceived the eagle and became king of the birds. We had our doubts, too, about the willie wagtail, which had three drops of the devil's blood on its tail, and so could never stand still.

Down by the tide there was a different set of birds, the oyster-catcher that was marked with a cross, the various gulls whose comings and goings were sure weather signs for those who could read them, the cormorants that sat on the rocks and spread out their wings to call the wind and the gannets reputed to be incapable of alighting on or rising from any rock except marble, and hence kept to the water nearly all of the time, laying their egg, we were told, on the surface of the sea and hatching it out by holding it between wing and body. And of course the swans on the Shannon; nobody would dream of harming a swan – weren't King Lír's children turned into swans, and who would want to take the risk of killing a king's child in disguise?

❖ Four-footed Neighbours

Among the wanderers on the roads of Kerry and west Limerick towards the end of the nineteenth century was a strange figure known as Coitir na Gruaige. A poet of some renown and a wild-looking fellow with a great bush of beard and long red hair which he wore in two pigtails, he scorned the humble gait and the outstretched hand of the ordinary tramp. Dressed in a coachman's great coat bound about with a leather strap he rode on a stout cob to the farmhouse doors demanding his tribute in a loud voice. If the contribution was satisfactory he called down blessings in verse; if he thought it mean or meagre his rhymed curses were heard all over the parish. Strangest of all was his power over rats. Once upon a time he arrived at a house in Cratloe when a party was in progress and with the usual hospitality strong drink was pressed upon him and he was requested to recite some of his poems. He had good head for drink but the liberality of the house was too much for him, and he finally fell into a drunken sleep, during which some joker cut off one of his plaits with a sheep-shears. Next morning he rode away and did not know of his loss until he dismounted at a roadside well to drink and wash his face, and found his pigtail missing on one side. Back on his pony he returned to Cratloe and as he passed each farmhouse by the road he called out some strange words and all the rats in that farm followed him, so that by the time he reached the partyhouse he had a great troop of rats behind him and these he ordered into the house and farm where they ate everything edible and ruined everything else.

And worst of it all was that nobody knew the charm necessary to drive the rats away. It is told of St Canice that mice gnawed his shoes and that he prayed against them and so drove them and the rats from his island hermitage forever. But nobody in Cratloe could pray to the same effect as St Canice and so they had to put up with the rats. But it's an ill wind that blows nobody good and farms from which Coitir drew the rats were free of them for a long time – until they had eaten the Cratloe people out of house and home. The elders who told us this story hated rats. Rats, they said, ruined everything they touched; they bored into the potato pits and took a bite out of every potato, and any potato they bite is poisonous from that on. Their burrowings let the rainwater into the pits. They befouled the oats so that no animal would eat it and if they got into flour or grain you might as well throw it out. And the cunning of them! You had to be something of an expert to trap or poison a rat, for they were suspicious of anything strange. Couldn't a rat bring an egg downstairs without cracking the shell? And didn't Dan the Cabbage see two rats leading an old blind one between them and the three of them holding a wisp of straw in their mouths? Mice were destructive enough, they ate all around them and bored holes in timber and tunnelled the thatch, but they weren't dirty and poisonous like the rats. Everyone's hand was against the rats, and only once ever did I hear anything good of them, from a farmer who held that they used the field drains as communication tunnels and so kept them free of obstruction.

The weasel, said the old people, was the boy to hunt the rats, and if you had the luck to have one living in your haggard there was no fear of your grain or potatoes. In actual fact there are no weasels in our district, or anywhere in Ireland for that matter, what we called 'weasel' is the red stoat. The local attitude to the 'weasel', as indeed to the fox, the badger and the otter was one of tolerance. If he left you and yours alone, then you left him alone. The 'weasel' gained some respect as a very brave, fierce fighter. He was very hard to kill and not many dogs would close with him, for no matter where the dog was gripped he could turn and bite the dog's face. If you killed a weasel all the others would gather from miles around and bury him; more than one of our neighbours claimed to have seen a weasel's funeral, and of course we all believed this. We were warned, too, not to attack one, for he could give a loud shrill whistle to call the help of all his friends. And it was no good trying to run away from them; they followed you for miles, creeping along by the hedges and fences and peering out every now and then to make sure they were on the right trail. And they had good memories, they could identify the person who had injured them even months later; they watched out for him and when they had learned where he lived they waited patiently until the chance of revenge came. He might wake one morning to find every fowl and every lamb on the farm dead, or they might spring at his own throat some dark evening and draw his blood. But for some unexplained reason it was held that a purse of stoat skin was very lucky, for it was never empty of money.

Once we caught a small hedgehog and tried to keep him as a pet. He grew quite tame and ate bran mash, worms and bits of meat out of our hands, but when we put him in the garden to keep the insects down he wandered away and we did not see him again. But we learned to know him as a gentle, harmless, amusing little beast – although with what seemed more than his share of fleas – and so we were not able to understand the attitude of many of the old people who disliked him heartily. They maintained that the 'porcupines', as they were always called, sucked milk from the cows' udders and that this injured the cows. And so the poor 'porcupine' was usually done away with on sight by being thrown into water, which made him unroll so that the dogs could kill him. One of our farmer friends told us that he had seen a fox crouched down motionless beside a rolled-up hedgehog; he watched unobserved for over a quarter of an hour until the hedgehog unrolled and the fox swiped with his paw. But the hedgehog was too wary and too quick, and the fox only got his paw full of spines.

There was no end to the stories which told of the cunning of the fox. They were quite common; they had been preserved by the landlords, and up to 1900 or thereabouts no tenant dared to kill a fox, although the hunt came very rarely to the district. After the land acts things changed and poor Reynard got paid with interest so that his numbers were greatly lessened. Wherever a fox's burrow was found it was dug out and its occupants set upon by dogs and killed, and thus many a raided fowlhouse and many a stolen goose were avenged. It was claimed that the fox, when he killed a goose, was able to sling it on his shoulders and so carry it off without trouble. If you found a dead fox, said the old people, you should make sure that he was really dead, for one of his many tricks was to pretend to be dead until the chance of escape came. We all had heard of the silly man that found a 'dead' fox in the hen-run and threw it out into the farmyard intending to pick it up later, and of how the fox was sitting on the wall making faces at him when he came out of the hen-run. And of the cleverer fellow who carried the 'corpse' into the kitchen and stood at the door with a slasher ready to kill. Whereupon the fox only bustled around the hearth picking up boots, socks and so on and dropping them on the open fire and in the rush to save his footwear the farmer let the fox escape. And, of course, the old, old story of the fish-hawker who added a 'dead' fox to his load, only to find, when he reached the village, that the greater part of his fish was gone as well as the fox. There was an old and very wily vixen that lived in a *cumar* not far from our house; she had had one paw caught in a trap and had gnawed it off so as to escape. We never heard of her being caught; many of the farmers' wives had fine fox fur boas; but the old vixen's fur never saw the inside of the chapel on a Sunday. Sometimes on a moonlight night she would give an extraordinary cry, mournful and weird and this helped greatly in keeping up the story of the *Bean Sidhe* and led members of certain families who had no claim whatsoever on the attentions of that good lady to pride themselves on having heard her lamenting, for the *Bean Sidhe* cried only for families of noble blood.

Another story told how a fox and a wolf made a tunnel into a fowlhouse, killed the fowl and settled down to a hearty feed. In a little while the fox excused himself and went outside 'to see if the farmer was coming', he repeated this several times, while the lazy wolf stuffed himself with tasty chicken. After a while the fox stayed outside and escaped when the farmer came, but the wolf, swollen with guzzled hens, got stuck in the tunnel and so was killed. The fox had gone out after eating each chicken to be sure that he was still thin enough to get through the tunnel, and when he found that it was a bit tight he stayed outside. There were other animal stories told in the locality in which the wolf played a part; the wolf was not regarded as a mythical beast or one known only in distant lands, but as a former inhabitant of the woods and hills, and the local tradition was that the last wolf was killed in Glendarragh, some five miles from Newcastle West, about 1750. As to the fox, only one animal was held to be his match in cunning, namely the 'wild cat', by which was meant the occasional domestic cat run wild, for true wild cats have not been seen in Ireland for a very long time. We were told of a talk between the fox and the cat, when the fox boasted of his cunning in escaping and the poor cat had to confess that he knew only one trick. Came the hounds and the huntsmen, and the cat did his trick – climbing a tree – while the fox, in spite of all his wiles, was run down and killed.

The badger was held in some respect and for the most part was left alone unless blamed for killing fowl. Not as cunning or as wary as the fox he more than made up for lack of wit by solid strength and courage. In former times he was hunted for sport in our district, but this practice had long come to an end. Some of the farmers liked to see a badger in the potato-gardens, holding that they loved to eat weeds but would not touch the potato-plants. And we were told that the badger never dug his own burrow, but found a home by evicting a fox, for the fox was afraid of him, and the badger always got the upper hand if a quarrel began. Witness the tale of St Ciaran who went to live as a hermit in the wood and was helped by the animals who formed a small community with the saint as abbot. But the fox grew tired of virtue and stole away the saint's hoes, to eat at his leisure, whereupon the indignant badger took the malefactor by the ear and marched him back to the saint, to do penance and be forgiven.

There were otters – we called them 'water dogs' – along the river still, but the old people spoke of two other creatures as having only recently disappeared when the last of the old woods were cut down, the squirrel and the marten; the latter remembered as the fiercest of all the wild creatures. Of hares and of rabbits there were plenty. The landlords had preserved the hares for coursing and hunting, although one landlord, Goold, had given the people permission to kill hares in the famine years, and we are told that very many hares and rabbits – which were not preserved at all, but killed off as destructive vermin – supplemented the people's diet in those hard times. In our district the hare was the game animal, and was never killed in any way except by hunting with dogs, either free or in the coursing field. To shoot or trap a hare was almost as reprehensible as to shoot or trap a domestic animal. Of course if you came out early on a May morning and saw a hare milking one of your cows you could shoot it, for it really wasn't a hare at all, but an old *cailleach* who had taken the shape of a hare so as to get some milk to make a charm to steal your butter. We all knew the story of the farmer who shot such a hare and followed it up until it ran into a little house where he found an old woman bleeding of the gunshot wound. But people were welcome to kill rabbits in any way they could, and these destructive little creatures were snared, shot, chased with dogs and driven out by smoke, water or ferrets. Rabbits were eaten stewed or roasted, sometimes stuffed like a chicken, and were somewhat of a titbit. Once, in the south west of County Kerry, I was much surprised when out shooting rabbits, for on offering one to an old lady of the place I was told that the rabbit was a sort of rat and that it could not be eaten by humans. We never ate the flesh of the hare; hare soup was relished, but the tough dark meat was disliked. The old people told us that in their young days the small boys often wore caps made of the skin of rabbits or hares, furry side out, lined with cloth, sometimes with the ears still attached, while cushions and chair-covers were also made of rabbit and hare skins.

❖ The Cricket's Song

People liked to hear the crickets chirping in the hob of the hearth. So much did they feel that the crickets were lucky and that no house was a home without their song that a few crickets were captured and brought into a new house so that they might settle down there. In any pause in the conversation around the open hearth at night, the cricket's song was heard, and a traveller on the road later at night could hear them as he passed the houses. Nobody dreamed of harming a cricket – even the cat knew better than to kill one of them. If you did kill or hurt one of them, the luck left the house at once and the crickets came out in full strength during the night and ate holes in your clothes. And they knew well if it was a person from outside the house who had done them harm; they followed such a one to his own house, and there joined forces with his own crickets to take revenge. They knew, too, if they had been hurt by accident; if you weren't too careless they forgave you, and all was well. In the dark of the night they came out on the kitchen floor, and quite a lot of people had the custom of leaving a bit of bread or a cooked potato on the flag of the hearth for the cricket's supper. When one of them died, the others held a funeral; four of them carried the body while the others walked in procession behind. Now all this is passing, for the cricket can find no home in a concrete wall and so they are not found in the new houses.

Far different is the *cleag*, the cockroach, a dirty, smelly beast, hated by everybody for his nasty habits and slaughtered without compunction. But they are horribly wary. When the candle was blown out in the farmhouse kitchen they came out on the floor and could be heard scurrying about; the moment the light was lit again they vanished into their holes like dark streaks. Frequently people poured boiling water into the cracks that harboured them, but always some survived. There was a man in our district who boasted that his house, although an old one, was always free of them, and some ill-natured joker slipped two live cockroaches into his pocket, and you can imagine his dismay when he pulled out his handkerchief in his own kitchen and saw the two horrors falling to the floor. By a quick jump he killed one with his boot, but the other got away, and he sat up all night, constantly lighting and quenching the lamp in the hope of seeing it, and at last saw it darting under a wooden peck on the floor. So much afraid was he that it might escape that he laid a ring of live embers from the fire around the peck before he lifted it, and the wretched cockroach was incinerated in its rush to escape.

Even less mercy was shown to the *dúradaol*, the devil's coach horse, for isn't he in league with the devil, and didn't he try to betray the Infant Jesus to Herod's murderers? Our Lady and St Joseph were hastening with the Child towards the safety of Egypt and passed through a field where the people were sowing corn. 'If the soldiers come, we'll tell them that nobody passed,' said the sowers. 'You must not tell a lie for our sakes,' said Joseph. And the next day when the soldiers questioned the workers, they had to admit to seeing the fugitives while they were sowing the corn. But when the soldiers turned to look at the field they saw it waving ripe, ready for the mowers, grown miraculously in one night, and they were moving away to search elsewhere when the *dúradaol* rose up with the shout of '*Iné, iné!*' – 'Yesterday, yesterday!' '*Bréag, bréag!*' – 'a lie, a lie!' called out the *ciaróg*, the winged black beetle, hoping to save the situation, but it was too late, the soldiers were already away in pursuit. On this the workmen fell upon the *dúradaol* and slew him. And ever since that time, it is a good thing to kill the *dúradaol*; some people said that he must be cut into seven pieces with the nail of your thumb, and that, by doing so, you'd never have the misfortune to fall into any one of the seven deadly sins.

We were often warned of the dangers of falling asleep out in the open, especially on a warm day, for a lizard might come that way and creep into the sleeper's open mouth and down his throat into his stomach. And sad was the plight of anyone who had such misfortune, for the lizard sat there in his stomach, and as often as he ate and as much as he ate, the lizard gobbled it all down, and the person's hunger was as great as ever. We were told of a man in a neighbouring townland who had been this afflicted. He put away the most amazing quantities of meat, bread, potatoes, sour milk and porter, but all to no good, his hunger grew more cruel until the poor man was nearly off his head with the dint of it. Then came the *bean feasa*, the wise woman, and ordered that no bit of food must he get for three days. "'Tis little difference 'twill make to himself,' said she, 'but 'twill annoy the *buachaill* inside in him.' On the fourth day she directed that the sufferer should be hung up by the legs from a rafter in front of the hearth. Then she put a pan of juicy porksteaks to cook on the open fire, and it wasn't long until the lizard smelled the meat and jumped out of the man's mouth to get it, and while it was guzzling the meat a large iron pot was turned over lizard, meat and pan, and a large fire built about it and kept going until the lizard was in ashes. Another story told of a holy priest being called to expel a lizard from a man's stomach. He read prayers from his book and at a certain point warned all present to close their mouths, for the lizard was about to jump out. One little child, however, too small to take the warning, kept her mouth open and in went the lizard, but, since she was completely innocent of all sin, the monster had to jump out again, and this time the bystanders made no mistake in killing it. If you touched a lizard, said the old people, it would break in two, and the parts would join together again during the night. But a child who licked a lizard would never burn its mouth, no matter how hot the food or drink, and, moreover, could cure the burns of others by licking them.

Only a few people in the district had hives of bees, and most people feared to go too near the hives, in dread that they might be stung. The modern, wooden hive was the type used, but down near the Shannon many farmhouses had rows of the old straw hives and plenty of honey. If any member of the family died, somebody had to go to the hives and tell the bees, and hang a little piece of black cloth on one of the hives as a sign of the bees' mourning. If this was not done, the bees were sure to swarm away at the first opportunity. There were three kinds of wild bees, the 'black bee', the 'brown bee' and the 'red-tail bee', of which the first two were common and the last rare. Often a *cnuasóg*, a wild bees' nest was laid bare by the scythe or the mowing machine, and the children braved the stings to come at the small store of honey, and the antics of a young dog seeing one for the first time were a source of amusement. Do what you would, the pup had to investigate; stop him now and he'll poke his nose into the next one. But once is enough, one sting in the sensitive nose and never again will he go near a bees' nest. The sting of the smaller brown bee was considered much worse than that of the big striped black bee, but neither of them as bad as that of the wasp. If a pup or any other animal went near a wasp's nest there was a rush to save it, as the wasps stung and stung again and could kill an animal or a child. Wasps' nests were destroyed, usually by fire; there was some honey in them, but of a poor grey kind which nobody would think of tasting. We were told that the only creature to brave the wasps was the *córnach*, the hooded crow, which was said to break up the wasps' nest and eat the honey and the grubs. The ant was held up to us as a model of industry and we heard the story of the silly grasshopper who wasted the summer days in singing and dancing instead of storing food and making a house and who appealed for shelter in the winter to the ant and who was told to dance to keep himself warm. Once when an ant's nest was revealed by the lifting of a stone and we saw the ants carrying the white grubs to safety, an old man pointed the moral by saying 'look at them now, will you, and everyone of them running with his own bag of provisions!' A swarm of winged ants in the evening was taken as a sign of rain. 'Water flies' running about on the top of the water in a pool or well also betokened rain to come, and some children tried to keep them in a jam-jar as a weather-glass. A swarm of midges in the evening was another sign of rain; otherwise the midge was held to be the most useless thing, only created by God to plague the builders of the Tower of Babel. Another weather-prophet was the frog; if fine weather was to be expected his skin turned yellow, but on the approach of rain he became dark brown, almost black. Nobody would deliberately kill a frog and people were sorry to see one killed by accident; we were never told why, but there was a feeling that they had some vague connection with the fairies. Most country children put some frog spawn in a jar of water in the spring to watch the development of the tadpole, and the old people told of jars of leeches kept in the houses long ago and used for bleeding sick persons. It was healthy, they said, to lose a little blood from time to time, and there was no harm in the bite of the 'doctor bee', the blood-sucking horsefly of which the children were so much afraid.

Fleas were heartily disliked. The tale was told of a *spailpín* who got cheap lodgings in the town, and had a loud complaint for the landlady in the morning. 'A flea in my house? Whist, boy, there is not a single one in it!' ''Tis true for you ma'am, for 'tis married he is, and with a long family.' Nest morning she said 'You were all right last night, and I having that flea killed for you.' 'You had so, ma'am, and what was in the parish of them came to the wake,' said the boy, moving to cleaner lodgings. Although disliked, the flea was often the subject of a joke or a funny story. But lice and bugs were regarded with utter loathing, a sign of the utmost filth and slovenliness, the mere mention of which was a slur and an insult. You might raise a laugh with the tale of how the fox got rid of the fleas by backing slowly into a river-pool while holding a tuft of wool in his mouth until all the fleas took refuge in the wool from the advancing water and the fox dived leaving the wool to carry its crew where it would. But the mere mention of lice, except in hushed tones was a sign of the lowest depravity, was as bad as obscenity or blasphemy.

Although people knew well that butterflies came from caterpillars, nobody would kill a butterfly, even the white ones whose caterpillars did so much damage to cabbage. Children often caught butterflies and put them in little rush cages but they always let them go again. Spiders, too, were not harmed, as their killing of flies and other insects met with approval, although the housewife had no mercy on the cobwebs. If a spider was seen to crawl upon a person's clothes this was a sign that he would get new clothes soon, for the spider is the skilful weaver and betokens woven stuff. Our only interest in earthworms was as fishing bait, but we heard that the seventh son of a seventh son had the power to kill worms by making a sign over them. On November Eve young girls used to get a slug and lay it on a plate sprinkled with flour, and in its crawling the creature would trace the initials of a future husband. And there was one tradition about snakes; because they had been driven out of Ireland long ago by St Patrick, the land of Ireland and everything that grew on it were proof against all manner of serpents, and anybody going from Ireland to a country where snakes lived should take a walking-stick of ash or hazel, blackthorn or holly, grown in Ireland, as a sure protection against them.

❖ 'TIS A WEDGE OF THE ELM...

Four hundred years ago Ireland was still a well wooded country. History tells of extensive forests and tradition remembers great stretches of trees on which a squirrel could go from Glenquin to Leabamolaga without putting a paw on the ground and there are boggy places where a spade thrust into the ground at any spot will strike tree roots. In the wars of Queen Elizabeth miles of woodland were cleared, lest they harbour the Queen's enemies, for the Irish had the unpleasant habit of using the woods as refuge and ambush, and of making things even more difficult by 'plashing', that is by intertwining the branches of the growing trees and bushes and sharpening the ends to make very formidable obstacles. When peace came many of the landowners, both old and new, took advantage of a growing shortage of timber in Europe and sold off great quantities of trees, especially oak. For nearly a century, it is said, most of the oil and wine exported from France and Spain was in casks made of Irish oak. It was believed, too, that Irish timber was not attacked by insects and was a protection against serpents, and it was much in demand for house building and furniture. Finally the small deposits of good iron to be found in many parts of the country were worked in little furnaces using charcoal as fuel, and hundreds of acres were burned. And so the woods were wasted until the day came when the poet lamented:

Cad a dhéanfaimid feasta gan adhmad?
Tá deire na gcoillte ar lár.
(What shall we do henceforth without timber?
The last of the woods are down.)

This meant not only the loss of timber. The native woods were useful as rough pasture for cattle as there were plenty of glades and clearings, and since the forests were mostly of oak, great herds of pigs could feed upon the acorns. We can be sure that the passing of the woods meant the loss of familiarity with trees and of many forms of skill and woodcraft. Such things as wooden houses and fences became extinct and the woodland animals and birds, the deer, squirrels, martens, the jays and black cocks disappeared entirely or survived only in a few corners. Even the climate was affected; there was less shelter and more damp, and life must have been much less pleasant for a lot of people than when the friendly forest offered all sorts of useful things.

Luckily there were parts of the country where trees remained plentiful, growing singly in the fields or fences, or in small groves or shelter belts. In the middle ages the farmers of the Pale were ordered to plant ash trees on their fences so that timber for the making of bows and arrows could be had, and trees in the hedges provided useful shelter for crops and cattle. More recently the habit of tree planting is spreading and there are districts bare of trees fifty years ago which now look well wooded, so many shelter-belts and groves have been planted; much of this comes from the time immediately after the land acts, when at last the farmers felt free to improve their holdings.

The oak was the king of trees. There was nothing, said the old carpenters, that you could not make out of oak, from a church roof to a child's top. The hedge schoolmaster made ink from the 'galls', the housewife made a brown dye from the sawdust, the tanner used the bark to cure leather. It was between the bark and the wood of an oak tree that the priest bound the Spirit of the *Beárna* for some horrible crime and there she remained for twenty-seven years until an unlucky flash of lightning struck the tree and released her; she killed several wayfarers and injured others before another priest overcame her and sent her to teem the Red Sea with a bottomless cup.

''Tis a wedge of the elm that splits itself,' says the proverb, and anybody who has worked elm knows how tough it is. That toughness has its uses and the carpenters, turners and wheelwrights knew them well, in making various things, such as coffins, wooden bowls, pump-barrels, wheel-stocks and – of course – splitting wedges. A poultice made of the leaves soaked in hot water was used to reduce swellings.

On the road from Newcastle West to Rathkeale an old ash tree is a conspicuous landmark. This is the 'Crooked Tree', for a long time used as a public gallows and even yet there are people who are nervous when passing it at night, in dread of what they might see there. Another ash tree on which two suspected Whiteboys were hanged at Sinan's Gate on the Glin side of Athea is said to be haunted too, and we hear of men travelling that road by night who saw the ghostly forms swinging in the moonlight. The ash tree is commonly found in churchyards and at holy wells, and it is said that a fire of ash will banish the devil. Whether this be true it is one of the few woods which will make a clean fire while green and newly cut. For furniture, wooden implements, tool handles, harrow pins and dozens of other uses, ash had no equal.

The old people said that if you rubbed a slug to a wart and then impaled it on a whitethorn bush, the wart was banished. If that were true, then few people would have warts, for any gardener will know how numerous slugs are and you find white-thorns in profusion wherever you go. The whitethorn is much more useful growing than cut, which is just as well, as you cannot always be certain that the bush you are going to cut is not a favourite abode of 'them that does be in it' and many is the story of what happened to people who cut the wrong bushes. There was a well-known herb doctor who reduced his patients to a proper frame of mind by consulting a lone whitethorn as to the necessary cure and we are told that the bush replied in a squeaky voice. 'Ventriloquy,' said the wiseacres; ''twas the power that he had,' said the more credulous. The blackthorn does not make so good a hedge, and it spreads out into the fields if it is not cut back. The sloes were used to flavour *poitín* in the old days, and children still try to make 'sloe wine' by putting sloes with sugar in a bottle of water and burying the bottle in the ground; the failure of this experiment is always put down to the fact that small people usually haven't the patience to wait the required number of months or else forget where the bottle was buried. Many an old ring fort is thick with blackthorns, and we are told of the famous faction fighter who was never beaten until his eye lit on a splendid blackthorn stick growing in a fort and he had the temerity to cut it. He sallied forth to the pattern of the village and challenged an old rival but when he raised his stick on guard it was as heavy as lead in his hand in spite of all his expert shaping and seasoning, and his enemy felled him with a single blow.

Another favourite walking-stick material was hazel. There was a robber once who had a stout hazel cudgel wherewith to batter his victims, until one day he came to a ford on the river and there was a man up to his waist in the water holding a hazel staff in his hand. The robber was told that this was a holy hermit who had vowed to stand there until God would grant him a sign that he merited Heaven, by causing the staff to sprout green leaves in his hand. Astounded at such piety the robber repented his evil life and joined the hermit in the river, and next morning his cudgel was growing green leaves, for his repentance was sincere and there was no pride in his heart. The robber came out of the river and spent the rest of his life in good works, leaving the hermit to reflect upon the wonderful ways of God. Hazel walking-sticks have other strange properties; they protect their owners against fairies and cure snake-bites, both claims difficult to disprove in a country where the fairies remain invisible and snakes do not live. For heavy wattlework, flail handstaffs, water divining forks and homemade fishing rods, hazel had no equal.

Elder is seldom found far from human habitation, and it is said that it has been spread by deliberate planting. In the old days it was highly regarded as a medicinal plant. The wood cured warts, the leaves made a poultice, clay from the roots cured toothache and the berries were fermented to make a palatable wine which was a good cough cure. Cleared of the soft pith the twigs made useful tubes, often converted into whistles and flutes or little cases for needles. Once upon a time, says the story, the elder was a fragrant, sweet-smelling tree, until Judas hanged himself on it, and from that day out it has an unpleasant smell, and if anybody deliberately strikes an animal or a child with an elder twig the animal will die and the child will grow no more.

Holly, with its bright leaves and red berries in winter when other trees are bare, was always loved as a Christmas decoration and a 'Wren bush' on St Stephen's Day. Small bowls and cups were turned from holly and its tough branches made walking-sticks, tool-handles and flail strikers. A t-shaped piece, with a short thick head and a projecting handle, made a strong durable mallet. It was boiled to make birdlime, and holly leaves under the pillow made a girl dream of her future husband.

Furze had many uses. Its strong stems made walking-sticks and hurleys. It was pounded and fed to cattle and horses. In many districts it was used to clean chimneys, a large bunch of it being pulled up and down the chimney by a rope. Spread under the cattle it made bedding and added bulk to the manure heap. Its blossoms made a yellow dye and it was cut and dried for fuel.

When the butter did not come in spite of careful churning the milk was stirred with a twig of mountain ash, or a band of the same tree was tied about the churn, for it was powerful against all sorts of charms and spells. The cattle drover who urged his charges on with a twig of mountain ash need not fear the ill effect of the evil eye, and a sprig in a fishing-boat brought luck to the fishermen. We are told, too, that it was used in evil magic; a wreath of its foliage or a withy made of its twigs was tied to a gatepost or a chimney to steal away the farmer's produce or bring misfortune upon his household.

Many farmhouses had a sally garden with willow rods for basket-making and thatching scollops; the purple osier was the favourite cultivated type. The black sally which grew wild in brakes and on fences was less valuable. Its bark was used to cure headaches and its ashes made into ointment; when laying down a clutch of hen eggs the housewife marked a cross on each egg with a charred sally twig, and small children suffering from hernia were passed through a hoop of split sally in the hope of a cure. Its wood was used sometimes for small pieces of furniture and for tool-handles. It was to a black sally that the barber of King Lavara Loinseach told the dreadful secret of the king's ears; he had been spared by the king on swearing that he would tell no human being, but was so troubled that he had to tell, and was advised to tell a tree. Then came the king's harper for wood to repair his harp, and behold! when next he played before the king the harp sang out for all the court to hear, 'The king has horse's ears! The king has horse's ears!' and so the secret was revealed to all.

The lordly beech, which is only a recent comer to Ireland, has gathered little tradition, but is prized for its good shelter and its useful wood. The lime is rare in most parts of Ireland, but in parts of Leinster was a favourite wood of turners, and its blossoms were said to give the very best honey. The alder's wood was held to be unaffected by water; it kept rats away and provided a good black dye. The yew is said to be the longest lived tree; the great yew in Muckross Abbey is held to be 900 years old, and some years ago there was difficulty in getting men to trim it as it is one of the trees which must not, according to tradition, be cut on any account, and we are told of a soldier of Cromwell's army who cut some of it for firewood, but was so shocked to see blood flowing from it that he fell dead on the spot.

Not every tree can boast of a life as long as that of the Muckross yew but a tree's life spans many human ones. Trees which were a familiar part of our great grandfathers' landscape are still part of ours, familiar neighbours, almost friends, and there are few of us who have not been saddened when one of these friends is blown down by a storm or felled for its timber.

❖ The Hungry Grass

In making the bargain with their employers the servant boys
and girls in our part of the country always claimed certain days
as holidays and foremost among these were the three days of the
big autumn race meeting in Listowel. It so happened that an
honest boy who was working for a farmer from the Knockanure
side borrowed his master's horse and car and jogged along to the
races, by Gortagleanna and Bolton's Cross and down Church
Street to the square where hundreds were gathered, some of them
making their way to the Island racecourse, some of them doing
the sideshows. There was plenty to look at and all sorts of ways to
spend your money, between the lemonade and the gingerbread, the
seagrass, the pies and the ported, the thimbleriggers, the trick-o'-
the-loop and the three-card men. And the biggest crowd of all was
out in the middle of the square, with their eyes as wide as saucers
and every 'Sabhála Dia sinn!' out of them with the wonder. The
boy from Knockanure couldn't make out what was going on at all;
he stood up in the cart on top of the sack of hay he had brought
for the horse. 'Yerra, what looking have ye?' said he, 'and nothing
to be seen except an ould cock and he tied to a traithnín of straw!'
'Excuse me, boy, but would you take a shilling for the sop of hay?
My pony hadn't a bite since last night,' says the man with the
cock. The bargain was made and the bag of hay passed out of the
cart. And there was the wonder, for when the boy looked again,
wasn't the cock pulling a huge beam of a tree after him? Magic, of
course, put in the eyes of the crowd by the man with the cock, and
he was quick to see that there was a four-leafed shamrock in the
beartán of hay; he knew well, of course, that the person who holds
a four-leafed shamrock is immune from charms and spells affecting
the eyesight.

If the four-leafed shamrock was lucky, the hungry grass was quite the opposite, and very unlucky indeed was he who trod on it. I well remember the night when a small brother was nearly frightened out of his life by a bearded apparition loudly groaning at the window; this turned out to be an elderly person known as Dan the Cabbage (so called from his selling of cabbage plants), who had on this occasion been overcome with weakness and had barely the strength to reach the lighted window. A little food and a hot drink revived him, and he told us how he had been walking across the fields as fresh and lively as ever he had been, when he stepped on the hungry grass and on the instant was struck with a hunger so violent that he almost fell down and died on the spot. So it is with the hungry grass. It cannot be distinguished from other kinds of grass; it grows on the spot where some poor wretch died of starvation in the bad times, and when you step on it you too suffer the pangs of famine. Experienced men often carried a bread crust in their pocket as a precaution, for the smallest morsel of food banished the hunger pain. And so it was with our friend Dan; hardly had a mouthful gone down when he was as cheerful as ever, and entertained us with parish gossip and rambling anecdotes until bedtime.

There were many other wild growths with peculiar properties and uses. In damp places, such as the river banks, the *bainnicín*, as we called the Irish Spurge, grew in great yellow-green clumps. Its juice is corrosive, and was used to remove warts, but its more sinister use, not mentioned in public, was the poisoning of fish. Then, as now, there were poachers and poachers; while nobody except the water-bailiff was much perturbed by the taking of an occasional sea-trout or salmon with gaff or spear, there was general disapproval of the use of poison. Yet one heard of a case of river poisoning sometimes, perhaps once in four or five years, when someone had filled a canvas sack with *bainnicín*, pounded the sack until the contents were beaten into a juicy mass and then dropped it into the river and every fish – eels, minnows, sticklebacks as well as trout and salmon – came floating dead to the surface for hundreds of yards downstream. Sometimes the poison affected miles of the water. This was rightly regarded as blackguardism and not as honest poaching.

Any man or boy going to the bog or the hill was requested by the womenfolk to bring back a bunch of heather for brooms and scrapers. For the housewife there were two kinds of heather, 'long heather' which made the brooms, and 'peck heath', the short stiff heath which was used for its colour and fragrance, and told the story of how it became such a handsome plant. Long ago, they said, when God was making all the plants and putting them growing in their proper places, no plant wanted to go to the cold, bare mountain, until the heather, then a humble, colourless growth, volunteered for the comfortless job and was rewarded by getting blossoms, scent and honey which set it far above the other, less obliging, plants. We heard, too, the tale of heather beer made by the Norsemen long ago, and how their lives and freedom were offered to the last two survivors – a father and his son – of the Vikings of the clifftop fort at Doon, near Ballybunion if they told how to make it. 'I'd be ashamed to tell, and my son listening,' said the old man, and so they killed the son. 'Now, ye can kill me too,' said he, 'for nothing will make me tell!' and they threw him over the cliff and the secret died with him. A great pity, said the old people, for, by all accounts, it was a wonderful drink, and it should be cheap to make with all the heather we had.

Very few of the wild plants were considered as food. Once in a while a person might pick up a bit of wood sorrel or watercress and chew it, but they never appeared on the table. Some of the older people kept up the custom of taking a dish of boiled nettles three times in the spring when the nettles were young and green; they had quite a passable taste, rather like spinach but it was for health reasons, as a renowned blood purifier, that the old people took them. They knew, too, that the *praiseach bhuí*, the charlock, is edible and told us how the poor people gathered it in the bad times and boiled it for food. The wild fruits were, of course, eaten. The favourite was the *fraochán*, the blue whorteberry that grew in profusion in the bogs, but the blackberry, the crab-apple, the sloe and the hazelnut were gathered and eaten, although there were doubts about the elderberry and nobody dreamed of tasting rowan berries. And of all the fungus growths, only the mushroom was eaten. Several plants were highly regarded as food for fowl and small animals. Chickweed, groundsel and the big purple thistle were chopped up and added to the hens' mess, and in the spring you often saw children and girls at the pleasant task of picking *castarbhan* (*hypochaeris radicata*) on ditches and dry banks for the same purpose. In the spring before it has flowered, this little plant looks like a small green rosette, but it was very difficult to pull as it has a long root, and the gatherers cut it with a small knife, usually a broken tableknife kept for the purpose, and this, with a canvas sack, was the gatherer's equipment. Often you saw two children, one on each side of a ditch working away with two knives and one bag. It took quite a long time to fill the bag, but it was a nice job on a warm day, and could be varied by picking primroses and cowslips and making daisy chains. It was too early in the year for some of the other games with flowers and plants, blowing dandelion clocks, catching bees in the fairy thimbles, making boats from *feileastrom* blades and plaiting bands and butterfly cages from rushes; little boys made whips and *bastúns* of the long soft rushes which grew in the marshy places. In the old days fresh green rushes spread on the floor was a sign of welcome to the guest; in our time this custom was long dead, but the memory of it was kept by the people who still spoke of 'spreading green rushes' before a visitor, meaning the giving of a hearty welcome. Rushes made candlewicks and rushlights, and were useful for cattle bedding and rough thatching, but their spoiling of the pasture land outweighed their usefulness. A certain west Limerick landlord, Goold, had a great horror and hatred of the fairy thimble, the purple digitalis, and ordered his tenants to eradicate it from all his lands. But by the 1920s it was flourishing again, and nobody worried about it although it was known to be poisonous; once we saw two young pigs and twenty-three ducks laid out dead in a farmyard because some careless person had mixed digitalis with their greens. People had a horror of poison. On that occasion the pigs and ducks were buried, as was any animal believed to have been poisoned, and many harmless plants were thought to be poisonous and therefore to be avoided.

Thistles, said the old people, grew only on good land, and they told the story of the blind man who set out to make a match for his daughter with the son of a farmer who tried to mislead the blind man on the question of the worth of his farm. The blind man and his servant boy came riding into the farm and when they dismounted the boy was told to tether the horses to two big thistles. 'But, sure, sir, there isn't a thistle in the field,' said the boy. 'If that's the way, *a gharsúin*, we might as well be shortening the road home, for we have no business with land that won't grow a thistle!'

One old woman, a neighbour and friend of ours, had been in her young days an expert spinner, and still had both blankets and sheets for which she had spun thread. She often told us about the making of cloth and of the way she used to dye the wool and linen yarn with locally gathered plants. The roots of the *bainnicín* gave black, *feileastrom* roots a grey-blue colour, brier roots a dark grey. Whitethorn leaves gave a dark blue and alder leaves a dark green. An expert could get a clear yellow from heather, but less skilful handling gave dull yellows or brown. The blossoms of furze and of *buachalán buí* also gave various shades of brown and dull yellow. Bright reds and blues were beyond the reach of those who depended entirely upon the local dye-plants, but could be got from madder and indigo; these had to be bought from the shop or, at an earlier time, from pedlars, and both these colouring stuffs have been known in Ireland and generally in western Europe for many centuries. The most difficult colour of all to get was bright green until modern dyes came on the market, but this did not worry the older generations; indeed, it was commonly held that bright green was an unlucky colour, especially for clothes.

There is a tradition that the *ceannabhán móna*, the bog cotton, was formerly spun and woven into cloth, and there is a long tale of a princess who made twelve shirts of the *ceannabhán* to free her brothers from a spell. Sometimes it was collected for stuffing pillows, if feathers were scarce. Ferns were burned and the ashes used in making soap; washing with fern soap was said to be very good for the complexion. The *misemín* (wild mint) and the *rileóg* (bog myrtle) were put with clothes and linen to keep the moths away, and they gave the cloth a pleasant smell. Dandelion leaves were dried to make a sort of tea, said to be very healthy, and *sponc*, used in the old days as tinder, was dried and smoked as a substitute for tobacco. Many other plants, too, had their uses, as food or drink, as medicines, as material for this and that. Nowadays all such things come from the shops, but rural life is so much less interesting for the loss of the old knowledge of plants, and their uses.

❖ CASTLES

You will find them dotted all over the country, for they are among the commonest of our ancient monuments, as well as being the most romantic. There surely are up to two thousand of them, if you take the whole of Ireland, although some counties have far more of them than others. T. J. Westropp made a list of 405 for County Limerick, and some of the other Munster counties are not far from that record, County Cork with over 300, Tipperary with 250, Clare with nearly 200. It was the Normans who began the fashion, and it is in the areas where their influence was most felt that the castles abound; Kilkenny has nearly 200 on record, Wexford more than 100, Mayo about the same and Galway over 250. The northern counties, into which the Normans did not penetrate, make a much poorer showing.

When Strongbow's tough warriors burst into the Irish scene late in the twelfth century, they knew well that their only chance of holding on was to build fortresses as quickly as they could. How well they built and how well they held on can best be told by the numerous Fitzgeralds, Lacys, Cogans, Prendergasts, Burkes and Berminghams still amongst us. And the local Irish lords were not slow to take the hint and set about building their own strongholds, and how well they took to the Norman fashion may be seen in many a fortress linked with the names of MacCarthy, O'Connor, O'Moore, Macnamara, O'Driscoll or O'Flaherty.

Before the coming of the Normans there was very little in the way of military architecture in stone in Ireland, although fine stone buildings of other kinds such as the churches and the round towers, were well known. Reginald's Tower in Waterford is held to be pre-Norman, and we hear of a few town walls, but otherwise the earthen bank and palisade was the main defensive work. That these could be formidable is clear from their remains, mighty ring-forts like Rath Meava, a mile south of Tara. The first wave of Normans brought in a new form of earthwork, the so-called 'Motte and Bailey'; this was a large flat-topped mound overlooking a larger, lower platform, each of these having heavy wooden buildings on them, and strong wooden fences or palisades around them. The wooden structures have now gone, but the mounds still stand. There is a fine specimen beside Newbridge College and another close to the main road at Cloncurry, between Kilcock and Enfield; other notable ones at St Mullin's, County Carlow, Kilfinane, County Limerick and Knockgraffon, County Tipperary are only slightly larger or better known than dozens of others.

But the Normans were not content with these earthworks, however imposing. They set about the building of castles, and it was in this early stage that the very biggest of them, the great military fortresses, were made. Probably the very first to be completed was Carrickfergus, just outside Belfast, which is ascribed to John de Courcy, the self-styled 'prince of Ulster', but other mighty strongholds like Trim, Carlingford, Limerick, Carlow and Nenagh are all from this early period of about 1200. Trim was the largest of all, a mighty castle by any standard. The great keep still stands nearly eighty feet high, with its main walls up to twelve feet thick. Still more remarkable is the huge curtain wall which encloses an area of more than three acres; this wall was over five hundred yards long and the greater part of it is still in good condition, with two of the great gates and five other towers. It was in one of these gate-towers that the twelve-year-old 'Prince Hal', later King Henry V, the victor of Agincourt, was left by his protector King Richard II when the latter left Ireland in 1399 after his ill-starred visit to the country. Limerick, another great fortress, is said to have been begun in the reign of King John; some claim that it was built under the direction of John himself when he was there, as a prince, in 1185.

These big military fortresses were under the direct control of the crown; they were the seat of the garrisons which held the land for the king – except, of course, for the times when they were in the hands of the 'king's enemies' in the varying fortunes of the old wars. But there are other great castles which were built by great and rich noblemen, like the Kildare Fitzgeralds, the Butlers of Ormond, the Burkes and the Desmonds. And lesser lords and chieftains followed the fashion as far as their means allowed – or as far as they could extract the wherewithal from their tenantry. In a country frequently disturbed by private as well as general wars, and with more than its share of robbers, both two- and four-legged, a strongly fortified house and bawn was a very useful thing to have; Fynes Moryson, who spent several years in Ireland as secretary to Queen Elizabeth's viceroy, Lord Mountjoy, tells us that the cattle were brought into the castle bawns every night as much from fear of packs of wolves as from the danger of thieves. And a handsome castle was a symbol of the owner's status and importance. Everybody with any pretensions to gentility had to have a castle, and – provided you were on the right side – there were 'housing grants' to be had even then. A statute of Henry VI, passed in the year 1429, provided this:

> It is agreed and asserted that every liegeman of our lord the king of the said counties (viz. Dublin, Meath, Kildare and Louth, counties of the English Pale) who chooses to build a castle or tower sufficiently embattled or fortified within the next ten years to wit twenty feet in length sixteen feet in width and forty feet in height or more, that the Commons of the said counties shall pay to the said person to build the said castle or tower ten pounds by way of subsidy.

In those days ten pounds was a lot of money.

Castles and fortified bawns continued to be built until shortly after 1600, but the coming of gunpowder really meant the end of them. The heavy guns that smashed the walls of Maynooth castle, the stronghold of Silken Thomas, sounded the death-knell of the castle, and in the following wars, under Elizabeth and Cromwell and in the quarrel between James and William, castle after castle went down before the cannon of the attackers. Many a castle surrendered as soon as the guns came up, for the defenders knew that it was only a matter of days before they went the way of the men who tried to hold Carrigafoyle or Glin or Dunboy against the new engines of war. As soon as the castle yielded the gunpowder was put to work again; a couple of barrels of it, properly places, blew down the gate or a corner of the wall, so that it could not be held again. Then the wind and rain, and the moss and ivy got to work and left them as we see them today, nearly all in ruins.

But what memories they hold for those who will stop and look. Red Hugh O'Donnell sliding down his rope to freedom. The mortally wounded MacGeohegan crawling towards the powder barrels with a blazing torch. Lady O'Moor dropping hives of bees on the attackers at Dunamase. Bishop MacEgan calling on the defenders of Carrigadrohid to hold fast and refuse to surrender and dying for his brave gesture. The three heads that Fr Peter O'Leary saw over the gate of Macroom castle. And where memory grows dim, you can be sure that legend steps in to fill the gap.

When Pierce Ferriter and his men stood to their guns on the walls of Ross castle their spirits were high. It might be the very last place to hold out against the Cromwellians, but wasn't it prophesied that it would never fall until a fleet sailed on the Lakes of Killarney? But the enemy leader had boats brought up the Laune, and there, one morning, was the fleet ready to attack. And so the garrison lost heart and the castle fell. At Carrignacurra, near Inchigeela, the wails of the slaughtered garrison may still be heard on stormy night; this tale is told of many castles, and other kinds of hauntings abound. At Ross castle beside Lough Sheelin, the ghosts are those of two unhappy young lovers who got caught up in the feud between their families, the Nugents and the O'Reillys. Castle Biggs, on Lough Berg, has a frightful spectre, a fire-breathing hound with cloven hoof, standing guard over a hidden treasure. The ghost at MacAuliffe's castle, near Newmarket, is that of a young bride who was mysteriously spirited away, none knew where, on her wedding-night, and that of Carrickogunnel an evil hag who holds up a light in an endeavour to entice ships on the Shannon to their doom. In some old war the Barry of Kildinan castle on the river Bride was betrayed to his enemies by a wandering shoe-pedlar who later paid the penalty of his treachery at the hands of Barry's faithful men. The pedlar was beheaded and his head stuck on a spike over the castle, and ever since then his miserable ghost wanders headless through the castle rooms. The gentle ghost of poor Sibéal Lynch still walks near Pierce Ferriter's castle at the end of the Dingle peninsula; Pierce had stolen her away from her people, and they were happy together until the day when her furious kinsmen surrounded the castle and Pierce hid her – out of harm's way, as he thought – in a cave beside the sea, only to find, when the danger was past, that she had been drowned by the rising tide.

Many a castle is said to be the original work of that notable builder, the Gobán Saor. We all have heard the story of how he outwitted the king of England who tried to kill him so that no finer castle could be built than the one just finished for himself. Some time later a squireen in County Kerry tried to improve on this; when the Gobán was laying the last stone on the battlement, the owner of the new castle pulled away the scaffolding, so that the builder was left on top with no way of escape. That is until a poor fellow reputed to be a half-wit passed by. 'Is it shtuck up there you are, Gobán?' 'It is, I'm afraid, Johnny.' 'Yerra man, didn't you ever hear that its aysier to throw down two shtones than to put up wan?' The hint was sufficient; a shower of stones and mortar showed that the Gobán had taken it, and the owner was quick with a ladder to release his captive before too much damage was done to his fine new castle. And so the tales go on. Ballymoy castle in Laois is swept by mysterious beings every Saturday. Castleconnel will fall, some day, on the wisest man in the whole world; it might be well for budding geniuses to avoid it! A good giant lived in Castlepook, near Charleville, and ground corn for all comers. In the dark of the night until some inquisitive oaf spied upon his work, when it ceased forever. At Ferns castle lived the beautiful but evil witch Cathleen Clare, who made a practice of enticing young men to visit her, and showed them to a bed which opened like a trapdoor and hurled them into a foul pit below. This went on until one lucky youth escaped, and the witch paid for her crimes, we are told, at the market cross in Wexford. A very large number of friends, many more than he could entertain came to visit the earl of Desmond on one occasion, and the poor man was in great trouble until he hit upon a plan to save his honour. He would take them all on a great hunt in the forest, and as soon as all were out of sight his faithful steward would burn the castle to the ground, so that he could face his hungry guests with a happy conscience. On his return, to his horror, the castle still stood firm, but, drawing near he saw rows of tables on the lawn, spread with a huge and magnificent banquet, for the faithful servant had summoned the debtors of his freehanded lord, and forced them to provide the means of spreading the board.

Legend would have us believe that many a castle was magically built in one night, with bullocks' blood in the mortar for good measure. The true story of their building and occupation in the stormy days of the past is no less exciting. So with legend or with history we are safe when we come to a castle.

❖ STANDING STONES

Visitors to Punchestown Races will know the long stone, the tall stone pillar that stands in a field close to the racecourse on the east side of the road from Kill. About thirty years ago this pillar fell down, but the soil is soft around it and it did not break, and it was put up again by the Board of Public Works and named as a National Monument. Experts came and examined the spot before the re-erection, and so we know a lot about it now. The pillar itself is twenty-three feet long, and with three-and-a-half feet of it underground it stands nineteen-and-a-half feet over ground level. It is over nine tons in weight. The examination of the site revealed an ancient grave at the foot of the pillar, thus it became clear that the stone was erected to mark the spot where some person of importance had been buried in ancient times. In other words, a tombstone.

Several other great stone pillars are to be seen within a radius of a few miles of the Punchestown long stone; Furness, Harristown, Longstone Rath, Craddockstown and Greta Connel all have stones similar in size to Punchestown, and that they were erected for the same reason, as gravestones, is shown by the fact that burials have been found at the foot of at least some of them. Incidentally, the Punchestown pillar was raised back into position by means of a pair of shear-legs and a winch with ropes and pulleys, an apparatus which might have been, and, indeed, very probably was, used by the people who first set it up two thousand years or more ago. We must not underestimate either the skill or the knowledge of our remote ancestors in carrying out feats of engineering or the amount of work which they were prepared to undertake. Some of the great cairns and burial mounds, like Newgrange or the Knocknarea cairn, contain many thousands of tons of material and must have taken years of work by hundreds of workers. At Browne's Hill, in County Carlow, there is a dolmen – a great monument like a stone table – of which the top stone, mounted on several other stones as legs, is estimated to weigh over a hundred tons, and although the Punchestown pillar, at about nine-and-a-quarter tons, is one of the largest of its kind in Ireland, there is a similar stone at Dol, in Brittany, which stands over thirty feet high and is said to weigh more than eighty tons. Even with modern apparatus the erection of such a mass of stone would prove no light task.

There are many standing stones to be found, singly or in groups, over the whole of Ireland. Of course not all of them are burial monuments, and not all of them are ancient. Witness the remark of the Kerry farmer to a group of antiquarians. 'Here is the *gallán* now for ye. Professor Hackenbush ascribes it to the Bronze Age, but me own theory, supported by that of me Uncle Jerry, *that quarried it and put it up*, is that it is a scratching-post for the cattle!' The original purpose of a monument of this kind may easily be forgotten, and such a simple pillarstone might be erected for one of many purposes, as a gravestone or a memorial to the dead, as a boundary mark, in memory of some great event, or for some practical purpose such as a gatepost or a scratching post, or be – although this is rare – of purely natural occurrence. Unless, then, there is some clear evidence such as the grave at the foot of the Punchestown long stone, it is usually not possible to say, from the appearance of the stone, what its original purpose was. And here, as usual, imagination steps in to fill the gap. There is nothing your intelligent countryman likes so little as a mental blank, everything must be explained and accounted for. And in the past, when historical tradition had run thin and when the connection between cause and effect was not fully appreciated, the explanation adduced – or invented – was often weird and wonderful. All sorts of events, probable and improbable, actual and imaginary, were recounted, and solid 'proofs' were not lacking. Near Highwood, in County Sligo, there is a great standing stone, eighteen feet high and eleven feet wide by seven feet thick. Geologists have shown that it is purely natural in origin, but that explanation would never do for our ancestors. Nobody could have put up a stone of this size, they argued, and so it simply must have some supernatural origin. And the tale developed of a giant who had a difference with a magician. The giant, poor silly fellow, was a strong believer in the efficacy of physical force, and went for the magician with malicious intent flourishing a large club. But the wizard, of a more subtle turn of mind, side-stepped neatly and caught the big fellow with his magic staff, turning him instantly to stone. The same wizard, or possibly a relative, was roused to action on another occasion by the theft of his cow. He chased the thieves, a man and a boy, and overtook them at Kilross, not far from Collooney, and his magic staff proved even more potent than he expected, for in striking the culprits he accidentally touched the cow, and all three, man, boy and cow, may be seen to this day turned to stone.

Nor, apparently, did the coming of Christianity make an end of this custom of petrification. For our early saints are likewise credited with passing fits of choler during which several miscreants were rendered harmless in the same effective way. When St Fiachna discovered that a dairy woman was stealing his butter he did not hesitate to loose a mighty curse against her, which turned not only herself, but her dairy and all her utensils as well, into stone. In proof of which they are still plain to be seen close to the saint's church at Teampal Fiachna, a few miles south east of Kenmare.

Seeing that so many of these stones are petrified people, it is not surprising that they show signs of animation at times. Some of them speak, others move about or dance. A rock in the parish of Davidstown, County Wexford, called the grey stone, was seen to go down to the river for a drink. And we are told that a boulder, known as the Mottey stone, which stands on a hill-top near Avoca in County Wicklow, goes down for a drink every May morning. The Mottey was once a woman, but for some misdeed she was turned to stone. We are assured that the Mottey stone has been photographed beside Tom Moore's tree, a good mile from where it usually stands. A pair of stones at Farranaglogh, County Meath, formerly had a very useful talent. They could be consulted, as an oracle and always gave true answers to rightly disposed people; they were especially famous for revealing the names of evildoers. If something had been stolen in the district, you had only to ask the stones, and they gave you the name of the thief and the whereabouts of the stolen property. Unfortunately the stones were sensitive about their dignity and worth; you must listen very carefully for the reply. And so it came about that some careless fellow insulted them by asking the same question twice, since when they are dumb. A great pillar in the parish of Kilnamartera, County Cork, is none other than Balor of the Evil Eye changed to stone. There was an old story that a crock of gold was to be found beside it and some men came to hunt for it, but were going home disappointed when a poor simple boy who was with them began to speak to the stone, which, to their astonishment gave answer. 'Big stone, where is the crock of gold?' said the poor half-wit. 'In the fort where the ash and rowan leaves fall,' said the stone. And so they knew where to look and found the gold. The most notable Irish-speaking stone, of course, is Cloch Labhrais in County Waterford, which always gave a true reply when consulted, but the message seldom brought joy to the listeners, because, as the stone never failed to point out, *is minic an fhírinne searbh*, 'the truth is often bitter'.

There are quite a number of pillarstones which have a hole cut through them. A standing slab near Doagh in County Antrim, with a round hole pierced through it was a trysting place for lovers; if they clasped hands through the hole it was a pledge of betrothal. Similarly a boy and a girl who touched fingers through the little hole in the pillarstone at Kilmalkedar church, near Dingle, had thereby pledged love and fidelity to each other. A holed slab in the graveyard at Castledermot is said to have been a swearing-stone; people took oath on it as they would on the Bible. Other holed stones had curative powers. If an infant was passed through the hole in the stone, called Cloch an Phoill, about two miles south of Tullow, County Carlow, the child was cured of rickets. In some cases it was only necessary to pull a cloth through the hole and the sufferer was cured. The banishing of warts by the use of water from a hollow in stone is well known.

Many standing stones carry carvings or inscriptions. One, at Turoe, County Galway, is covered with elaborate carving in a handsome pattern of curves and whorls; it is dated to the Early Iron Age, a few centuries before the birth of Christ. But the best known are the ogham stones, carved with inscriptions in the ancient ogham characters; there is nothing mysterious about these, as ogham is a simple code which may easily be read, and the inscriptions are no more than the names of deceased people commemorated by the stones. About three hundred ogham stones are known. Most of them are smallish, three feet or so high, although there are a few very large ones, like the great fan-shaped stone close to the site of Leitrim Barracks in the Glen of Imáil, County Wicklow, which incidentally was said to have been thrown by a giant from the top of Lugnaquilla – the ogham characters being advanced in proof of this as the marks of the giant's fingers. Some pillars are marked with a carved cross. A few of these are known to be boundary stones marking the limit of the lands of a monastery, or serving some obvious ecclesiastical purpose. Others are clearly Christian burial monuments. Some are carved in handsome patterns and a few have crucifixions or other figures cut on them, and these are regarded as the forerunners of the fine high crosses with their beautiful decoration and carved figures. But some of the stones marked with crosses are believed to be much older than Christianity in Ireland; they are said to have been associated with pagan worship and 'christianised' by the missionaries and monks of the early Church.

On top of the hill of Tara, close to the statue of St Patrick, stands the most famous pillarstone in Ireland, and every visitor to Tara should lay his hand on it. For this is the *Lia Fáil*, the stone of destiny, at which the high king of Ireland was proclaimed, and when the true successor to the throne placed his hand upon it, the stone gave a great cry. It will, says the legend, even now cry out if the rightful heir touches it, so all should try their luck, if only to enjoy the reaction of the public authorities when the oracle again proclaims a high king.

❖ WEE FOLK, GOOD FOLK

Nobody, not even himself, could ever guess why James Maloney, as sensible a man as you'd ever meet in a week's cycling, should be sitting – of all places – outside the big fort of Lisnashee – of all times – coming towards nightfall on May Eve. But there he was, sitting on the old wooden plough, drawing comfortably on his pipe and watching the last gleam of colour in the western sky. And that was an end to his comfort for a long time, for, as the last light faded the little people of the fort came pouring out like bats out of a cave, everyone of them jumping on a *buachallán buí* and shouting at the top of his squeaky voice 'A horse for me!' and the weeds changing into ponies as fast as you like. It may have been his natural desire to get something for nothing that prompted James, or it may have been the madness of the moment, but anyhow he joined in the chorus, 'And a horse for me as well as the next man, by herrins!', and with that the old wooden plough took off like a jet clipper leaving Shannon airport. A couple of hours later, after a bumpy crossing of the Bay of Biscay and bad icing conditions above the Cantabrian mountains, where should James find himself but in Spain, wooden plough and all. And it cost him a fair penny to get home again, not to mention what his wife said about it, for it is a far cry from Lisnashee to Andalusia; train fares don't grow on bushes and Mrs James had heard about the lovely señoritas of Seville and Granada. One thing is certain: James is not likely to be seen anywhere near the fort on May Eve again, or on any other eve for that matter.

It was a different story with Johnny Shannessy down near Foynes, when his winsome young wife pined away and died before they were half a year married. A wise woman of the place had her suspicions and took to watching the fort in the dark of the night and, sure enough, there was young Mrs Johnny riding with the fairy host. The wise woman knew a thing or two about the fairies. Indeed it was whispered that this wasn't her first dealing with them – not by a long shot. Anyhow she gave Johnny his instructions, and there he was the next night at the mouth of the fort, standing in a ring of holy water with a black-handled knife in his hand. Out came the good people and there was his wife side-saddle on a black horse, and before a fairy could lift a hand or a voice Johnny had her off the horse and inside the circle, after slashing the rope that bound her to the saddle. All the long night fairies danced with rage and yelled threats and curses outside the ring until the dawn came and the clamour died away. To this day neither Johnny nor his wife has ever again seen a fairy, nor have they any wish to renew acquaintance with them.

And so the stories go on. There was the man who joined in the fairies' hurling match and the hunchback who put another line to their song '*Dé Luain, Dé Máirt*' ('Monday, Tuesday'). There was the piper who learned the fairy music and the drovers who were entertained right well in a house that had vanished away when they woke in the morning stiff with the cold and covered with dew right in the middle of a fort. And there was the priest riding home after a sick-call who was stopped by a crowd of the little people with the question – were they ever going to have a chance of going to heaven? 'If there is,' said the good priest, 'in your veins as much as one drop of the blood of Adam, heaven is your heritage as well as mine.' With that they set up a mournful *olagón* that rang in his ears until the day he died, and vanished wailing into the night. So the stories go on, and all over the country you have people pointing to this place and that as the abode of the fairies.

First of all there are the forts, those circular enclosures with stout earth banks that are so common in nearly every district in Ireland. There may be as many as thirty thousand of them in the country. Some of them are great big fortifications, formerly military posts or the strongholds of chieftains and princes. But most of them are only the remains of the enclosures around the dwellings of the farmers of ancient Ireland, and they were built as much to keep out wild beasts, such as wolves, as to protect the family and the stock from human marauders. But tradition makes them the homes of the fairies and as often as not they are called 'fairy forts'. And so nobody should do them any harm or interfere with them in any way. The reluctance to harm the forts is one of the reasons why so many of them survive. Nowadays we have some respect for the past, and the historians and archaeologists can get a lot of valuable information from the examination of ancient remains, but this feeling of reverence for the relics of our ancestors is quite new, and in former times up to sixty or seventy years ago it would not hinder people from destroying them if they saw any profit in it. Many of them were destroyed. Forts were levelled, burial mounds were used as topdressing, castles and abbeys made convenient quarries of dressed stone, ogham stones made handy lintels for doors or windows and grave-slabs were turned into paving-stones. Most of this was done by 'improving' landlords and their agents; the ordinary country people were restrained by the old tradition that these places were inhabited by beings of the other world. In fact we may claim the fairies as the best protectors of ancient monuments the country has ever seen. But for them we should be very poor indeed in monuments of the past, especially forts and earthworks which are comparatively easy to remove and provide useful material. Even now there are rumours of bulldozers at work on some of them. Of course they cannot all be preserved, but – and this is a very important consideration – they should be seen by some expert before they are demolished. When we remember that the Ardagh Chalice, one of the most beautiful and valuable examples of precious metalwork ever made, was found in a fort, we may wonder how many precious and lovely objects have been ground into dust by the bulldozer.

Many of the forts have *souterrains*, that is passages or chambers underground, and these, says tradition, are the entrances to fairyland. Tales are told of people who ventured down and were never seen again. Once a piper went down; he is still straying through endless tunnels and the wailing of the pipes may be heard at the entrance. A boy crept down and peered through a crack into a room where the fairy ladies sat spinning. Back he went, full of his story but found that they had taken away his voice for fear he would tell of the wonders he had seen, and he remained dumb for the rest of his life. Another story tells of a farmer who decided to plough up the fort, but was not long at work when the ground opened and swallowed him, horses, plough and all; this tale may have started when a plough-team did actually fall into a *souterrain* on the site of an old fort. Most of the forts in the country were believed to have such underground chambers, and many of them were said to hold great treasures. Sometimes a daring treasure-hunter went and dug in a fort or a mound, but if he did, said the neighbours, he had no good of it; bad luck was sure to follow him, and even if he did find the fairy gold it was sure to turn into leaves or ashes before he could spend a penny of it.

Another haunt of the good people is the lone bush. Nearly always a whitethorn bush, it stands alone in the field; the cattle graze around it but do harm it and the little people dance and play around it all night. And woe betide the foolish man who cuts down a fairy thorn. Sometimes he gets a fair warning; the axe is lifted to strike when he sees his house on fire, and off home he runs to find that it is a false alarm. Often the little people are kind enough to give him a second chance and off he runs again to save his house, to find it unharmed. But the third time he ignores the sign and chops down the bush, and finds his house and all his byres and sheds laid in ashes when he returns home. Or the axe skids off the tree and makes a horrible gash in his leg. Or he puts a piece of the bush on the fire and it flares up and burns him. Or his crops fail and his livestock dies. And so the lone bushes still stand in many a field.

Some of the good people have a love for high places, and have claimed many of our hills for their own. Knockma in County Galway and Mweelrea in County Mayo. Knocknarea in County Sligo and Drong Hill in County Kerry. Knockfierna in County Limerick and Slievenamon in County Tipperary. The last named is the typical fairy mountain, *Sliabh na mBan bhFionn*, the mountain of the fair-haired women who, of course are fairy women. Many a tale is told about it. Long ago, when so many people went barefoot and there were no rubber wellingtons to keep the feet dry it was the custom in every farmhouse and *bothán* that people washed their feet at night. And somehow or other the good people had some power over the feetwater, which should always be thrown out and never left inside all night. Incidentally, when throwing it out the old people always called out *Seachain!*, 'beware!' to give warning to the fairies. Anyhow, it happened one night that the people of the house forgot to throw out the feetwater, and they were not long in bed when a voice outside said 'Open, feetwater!' and with that the door opened and in came a crowd of golden-haired women, every one of them as small as a twelve-year-old girl. Down they sat and began to spin and the thread simply poured out of the spinning-wheels, so that the people of the house were in no doubt as to who the little women were. At last one of the girls picked up courage and took a bucket and walked out, saying that she was going for some fresh water, and ran as fast as she could to the house of the bean feasa who told her exactly what she must do to drive away the fairy women. Back she came with her bucket of spring water, and then with a casual glance out through the window remarked, '*Ochón ó*, there's Slievenamon all on fire!' on which the fairy women grabbed up their wheels and ran from the house. Needless to say, the feetwater was never again left inside during the night in that particular house.

Many mounds, too, are inhabited by the good people. Some of them are artificial, ancient burial mounds or the mottes on which the Normans built their wooden watchtowers. Others are just natural, small hillocks. But our ancestors held that they were hollow, and that at certain times a doorway opened and the good people came out. Indeed there is a story about a woman who was kneading a losset of dough one day when a small woman walked in and, without as much as 'by your leave' lifted the three-legged pot from the fire and walked off with it. And in the pot was a good Irish stew, nearly ready for the men in the bog and the children coming home from school. When the outraged housewife got back her breath she set out after the little woman and caught up with her at the fairy mound. 'Oscail!' said the little woman, and the hidden door opened and closed again behind her. So great was the housewife's indignation that she was not to be daunted by any such unusual happenings. 'Oscail!' said she, and ran in and grabbed up her pot of stew from the fairies' fire and was outside again before they could raise a hand. The little people loosed their dogs, but the housewife delayed them by throwing them the mutton-bones from the pot, and so reached and crossed the stream of water on the field boundary, and was safe, for they lose their power when they cross running water. In many places the old name *sidheán* is still used for these mounds, and even still there is a great reluctance to harming them.

In travelling from one of their abodes to another the good people go along regular paths. And if anybody should dare to obstruct a fairy path, he would soon feel the disapproval of its owners. Worst of all was to build a house on a fairy path, for all kinds of ill-fortune plagued the unlucky occupants, from constant and horrible noises in the night to bodily injury to man and beast. The wise man made sure to select the site of his house with this in mind. One method was to go to the proposed site on a windy day and throw one's hat in the air. Then the good people recognised the honest desire to placate them, and blew the hat along to a site which did not hamper their movements, and there the house was built. Of course we have all seen the whirlwind, and know that the wind-fairies – the *sidhe gaoithe* – were out on their rambles.

And then there are the solitary fairies. For instance the *púca*, who lives in rocky glens and river pools, and appears in the form of a horse, trying to get people to climb on his back so that he can drag them away miles from home and finish by throwing them into a boghole. But the tale is told of how he met his match when a stout fellow, well equipped with whip and spurs, rode him so unmercifully that the poor old *púca* was glad to get back to his rocky lair and did not appear for several years afterwards. Still, it might be just as well to avoid strange horses in the neighbourhood of Pollaphúca, Gleannaphúca, Carrigaphúca and other places bearing that ominous name. Then there is also our old friend the *leipreachán*, a harmless poor creature who only wants to be left alone to cobble his shoes and watch his little pot of gold. Indeed, the Society for the Prevention of Cruelty to Helpless Creatures might well intervene in more flagrant cases of interference with this poor little fellow, who, after all, does more than his share of attracting American tourists to our shores. But far different is the *dallachán* and well may you avoid him, for he has the gruesome habit of appearing without any head, and, as soon as the fact of his headlessness has dawned on the mind of his unhappy audience, he puts his hand into his pocket and takes out his head, all dripping with blood, and glares for a moment at the cowering wretch in front of him before he returns it to his pocket and paces morosely on his way. Jackie-the-lantern (alias Willie-the-wisp) is another of these lone birds, although a fairly harmless one, for his attempts to lure strangers into the bog with his light, which he fondly hopes they may mistake for a candle in a window, have little chance of success since the coming of rural electrification. The poor chap never thought of increasing his candlepower; or maybe the effort is beyond him, especially since Pollaphúca has been forced to contribute to the rival show. All sorts of fairies, indeed, are hit by hard times nowadays. They become ignored and despised, disbelieved and disinherited. They are in sore need of some form of protection, and our humanitarians might well turn their eyes in their direction. Why not put them to work for the tourist trade? The least of them – the *leipreachán* – is already doing his bit, and with a little goodwill and give-and-take most of the others might be persuaded to join in with mutual profit and entertainment. For a start, what about a few carefully chosen and sited notice boards, such as those currently used to indicate the more prominent antiquities? Starting, let us say, with 'fairy mound, do not disturb', or '*dallachán*, don't look now', or 'beware of the *púca*', and gradually working towards bigger and better things.

❖ Water Monsters

One of our favourite rambles was down to the river by the Old Mill *bóthairín*, where we were often intercepted by an old lady full of dire warnings about the dangers of the deeper pools, especially one treacherous hole that had a mud bottom. 'And let you stay far out from that one, *a mhaoineach*, or maybe 'tis how the *seana chaoire adharcach* would come out of it and eat you!' we stayed far away from that one. Thoughts of deep water, currents, cliffs and other hazards of the river affected us not in the slightest. We fished in the pools and often fell into them, sailed *feileastrom* boats in the strongest currents, slid down the cliffs, but the thought of some muddy monster emerging from the boghole kept us well away. What fearsome shapes it assumed in the other children's imagination I have no idea, but I always pictured it as a savage version of Tenniel's picture of the Gryphon in *Alice in Wonderland*. Similar tales were told to other children in other places, and we may be sure saved the lives of more than a few. There was some horrible creature in the deep water of the dangerous place. It might be a beast, such as an eel or a serpent, or a human figure like the Boody Man or Oliver Cromwell, or as we hear from certain northern districts, even His Holiness of Rome.

There surely is some connection between these childhood fears and the tales, once so common, that peopled almost every stretch of water in the country with strange monsters. Along the sea-coast there was no need for make-believe, for the sea had its real monsters, as terrible as any imagining, the whales, sharks, and walruses that every fisherman had seen. But apart from a big salmon or pike, there were no large creatures in the fresh water. There were, of course, eels and otters, and both of these were suspected of more than ordinary activities. The eel, because of its resemblance to a snake and its habit of travelling over land on wet grass at night, was an obvious candidate for election to the ranks of water monster. On the Shannon, the Erne and other rivers, eels were captured in thousands for export, but very few Irish country people would eat eel; it is slimy and difficult to hold, difficult to kill, and addicted to feeding on carrion, and none of these characteristics endeared it to a people always choosy about the fish they ate. We heard nothing good about the eel except that its skin made fine thongs and razor strops. Otherwise it was not a nice neighbour. We heard of the big eel that came out of the river and ate a clutch of chickens and of the even more daring one coming into a kitchen and taking food from an iron pot and getting its head caught so that it took the pot back into the water. We were told that an eel could travel very fast across the country by taking its tail in its mouth and bowling along like a hoop, and of the many night travellers who only just escaped from these horrible pursuers. A small step farther in these tales brought one to the monster eels, twenty feet long or more, guarding treasure chests at the bottom of the lakes or in deep caves.

Then there is the otter. Generally a harmless creature – except for its destruction of game-fish – it defends itself bravely when attacked and so has a reputation for ferocity although a pet otter can be as gentle and affectionate as a collie pup. In our district, as well as in most parts of Ireland, it was generally called the water dog, and we were warned against its sharp teeth. We were told of the king water dog, a great beast with a white belt and black ears, the ruler of all the otters, and assured that its skin would give complete protection of the house in which it was kept against the danger of fire. Ordinary otter skins were highly thought of; some people had floormats made from them, and a skin buyer would give a nice price for them. People had some regard for the otter; he was, they admitted, a dangerous beast at close quarters, but not to be hated and despised like the eel. There was a tale of a man who shared his food with an otter, and was rewarded later when the otter came to his help by bringing him valuable things from the bottom of a deep pool. But there are tales, too, of monstrous, savage otters. In County Leitrim there is a story of how a lady went to bathe in Glenade Lough and was killed by a giant otter which claimed the lake as its own domain. Her husband, Terence MacLoughlin, arrived too late to save her but fought and slew the monster with his sword. In dying it gave a loud whistle and its mate, an even larger and more fearsome monster, rose from the depths to avenge it, but MacLoughlin and his brother sprang upon their horses and drew it away in pursuit, and when well away from the lake fell upon it with their swords and killed it after a fierce struggle. The tombstone of MacLoughlin and his wife, Grace Connolly, is still pointed out in Convall graveyard.

Many an Irish lake is reputed to have a monster bound in its depths by the prayers of a saint. Lough Curra in the Galtees is one such. A great serpent was ravaging the Glen of Aherlow until the good St Beircheart, whose *cill* and holy well are still places of pilgrimage in the glen, overcame it by his prayers and banished it forever to the depths of the lake. Another monster devastated the valley of the Shannon, until the inhabitants in despair turned to St Ciaran of Clonmacnoise and he went out against the monster with book and bell and drove it into the depths of Lough Ree. We are told that this *piast* is still seen swimming in the lake at times; it has been seen, as we learn from recent newspaper reports, not very long ago by parties fishing in the lake. Still another *piast* is in the Devil's Punchbowl above Killarney. Here the saint who exorcised it was, it is to be feared, guilty of some degree of prevarication, for he took advantage of the simple monster by a play of words in Irish, telling it to stay in the lake until *Lá an Luain*, which as we know, can mean either Monday or the Judgement Day; the monster understood the first, while the saint intended the second meaning, and so the poor monster was deceived. And we are informed that people walking by the lake still hear the melancholy question 'isn't it a long week until Monday?' echoing from the dark depths. Lough Derg, on the Shannon, is named from another monster, too insecurely bound by some novice. It broke its bonds and came on shore to resume its career of destruction, but made the initial mistake of swallowing one of the bodyguards of a local chieftain, and this stout fellow drew his sword and carved his way out. The flood of gore flowing from the dying monster turned the whole lake red, and hence the name.

One of the commonest types of lake monster is the *each uisce*, the water horse, these, if we are to believe the stories are to be found in almost every lake and large river pool in Ireland, and are often seen playing about on the surface, dashing the water on high to the terror of the passers-by, and these are well advised to hurry on their way and leave the creature to his fun. In Carrowmore Lake, in County Mayo, there is a water-horse which comes on shore and grazes in the fields, looking so mild and gentle that many adventurous youths have been coaxed to climb on its back. It then plunges into the lake and the luckier riders get off with a drenching. As to what happens the unlucky ones there is no telling, for none of them has ever returned from the depths to which the monster carried them. Not all water horses are unfriendly, however. We hear of a beautiful white mare coming out of Counfea Lough in the Comeragh mountains and working for six years on a local farm where she was treated with great kindness and became the pet of the whole family. Each year she had a foal as beautiful and as friendly as herself, and all would have been well, had a bad-tempered workman not struck her with a whip. Enraged at this insult she whistled to her foals, and the whole troop galloped back to the lake and disappeared under the water, never to be seen again.

A very famous water horse lives in Lough Nahanagan in the Wicklow Gap. Once upon a time a travelling scholar with a wicked sense of humour persuaded an old lady that a certain cure for her crippling rheumatism was to be found in the lake, and she got two of her farmworkers to mount a *súgán* chair on a couple of poles, like a sedan chair of old, and carry her up to the lake, where she sat awhile admiring the view while her bearers had a quiet smoke. Her wonderings as to what the cure might be were resolved by the sudden eruption of the horrible horse in the middle of the lake, and the workmen ran like hares. But, *mo léir*, didn't she pass them out before they were gone a half a mile of the road home, and, moreover, didn't she win the step-dancing contest at the local *feis* the very next Sunday?

There are water cows too. At certain times a herd of white water cows comes out of the depths of Lough Gur, in County Limerick, to graze in the fields. It is even said that in the bad times they allowed themselves to be milked by poor people of the neighbourhood. But water bulls are said to be even more dangerous than the land variety, and should be avoided at all costs.

Certain lakes have their own unique monsters. Under the gloomy cliffs of Com Shingaun, to the west of the road from Carrick on Suir to Dungarvan, a mysterious figure in the shape of a huge man covered with long hair comes out of the lake and wanders on the shore. Nobody has ever waited long enough to examine him closely. A great black shape has been seen breaking the wind-tossed surface of Lough Looscaunagh between Killarney and Kenmare, and another strange creature has been seen more than once in Lough Brin. A short while ago there was a report that a local sportsman engaged this monster with a shotgun, but failed to kill it. Taking all the known facts into consideration the first place among Irish lake monsters must be granted to the Carrabuncle. This extraordinary animal lives in a small lake in County Kerry. Anyone who has travelled from Dingle to Tralee over the Conor Pass will remember the small lakes in the *cúm* on the northern side of the pass. Even in bright sunlight they look deep and dark, and you might wonder why one of them is named Lough Geal, the bright lake. But its brightness may be seen only on the nights when the Carrabuncle comes out of the depths to swim near the surface. He is a great creature, bigger than a bull, and studded all over with every kind of jewel and precious stone, and it is the glitter of these which make the lake shine like the moonlight. We know little about him, for nobody has braved the rocks and the bogholes to wait on dark nights by the edge of the lake and see him near at hand. Indeed it must be admitted that few of our lake monsters have ever been properly investigated. Who knows what secrets may be revealed to the enquiring mind which will devote itself to their study?

❖ THE BUTTER STEALERS

There is hardly a parish in Ireland where the story of the hare that steals milk is not known. It tells of a farmer walking out in the dew on a May morning with his dog and his gun, and seeing a hare sucking milk from one of his cows. The hare ran, the farmer shot at it and the dog went in pursuit. The hunt led away across the fields to a little old house wherein dwelt an old woman, and there the farmer found her lying on the floor bleeding from a gunshot wound. For it was she who had gone in the form of a hare to take some of the cow's milk and so get the magic power to steal the butter from that farmer's dairy from that until the next May day. This was a serious matter, a threat to the farmer's livelihood, for butter was much more than a garnish on the kitchen table; it was an important item in the farm economy, a major source of income. If, for any reason, a churning failed, or if the butter was tainted or of poor quality, it meant so much less for sale on the next market day, and if this happened repeatedly and all natural means failed to remedy it, there were dark suspicions of charm-setting butter stealers. Dozens of stories were told about the activities of these miscreants and many people believed that their power was something more than natural.

There were many ways of setting these charms. Milk stolen from the cows and put in the stealer's churn meant that an abundance of butter came from it while the victim's efforts produced only a churnful of froth. Often at milking time a cow's feet were tied with a 'spancel' and many of these were made of cow-hair; such a spancel could be used to work most potent charms. Hung from a rafter with suitable incantations it dripped cream into a pan while the cream in the dairy of the farm from which it was stolen grew less and less. Once upon a time, we are told, a servant boy came to his master and told him how an old woman had offered him a golden sovereign if he would steal a spancel from the byre, dip it in one of the cream-keelers in the dairy, and bring it to her. The master told him to take the spancel, to dip it in the cesspool and then hand it over and get his sovereign. And so he did, and the curses and lamentations of the old woman were heard over three townlands when filth flowed from the spancel into her churn. Another tale of the spancel relates how a priest was returning from a visit to a sick parishioner at daybreak and saw a woman drawing a spancel over the morning dew and chanting 'come all to me!' For a joke, and to give her a scare, the priest called out 'and come some to me, too!' Later on the same day his housekeeper came to him in a dreadful fright, for no sooner had she begun to make the priest's little one-cow churn than a flood of butter poured from its mouth. It was then that his reverence realised that he had, unwittingly, become a partner in the spell, and it took many days of prayer and fasting before he was delivered from the plague of unwanted and unhallowed butter.

If anyone came into the kitchen or the dairy where the churn was being made, he or she must at least lay a hand upon the churn-dash or the handle so that, having taken part in the work, he or she could not steal the butter. And to ask for the loan of anything during churning was the worst of bad manners because it meant that the people of the house must refuse the request, as nothing, not even a drink of water or a light for a pipe, must be taken from the house during churning. Even the beggars who came to the door knew they must ask for nothing until the churning was finished. Indeed, the milk, the cream and the butter were vulnerable from the time of milking until the firkins of butter were taken away to the market, and there were many counter-charms. Some people relied upon prayer and the blessed things such as the St Brighid's cross which hung in the byre, the holy water sprinkled on the cattle at Easter, the singeing of the cow's udder with a blessed candle, but others used forms of protection which may have been old when Christianity first came into the West. A red coal from the fire was dipped in the churn or placed under it, or a piece of iron was made hot and used in the same way. And salt had great merit; a pinch of salt preserved most things against evil magic. Twigs of roman or of elder hung in the byre gave security and a silver coin placed on the cow's back during milking kept evil away; some said that this must be a florin (which, in the old days, had a cross pattern on its reverse side).

When butter-stealing was afoot there were many ways of discovering the culprit and forcing him or her (usually her, according to the stories) to desist and make restitution. In most cases it was necessary to get help from someone with uncanny powers, such as the *bean feasa*, the wise woman. Often the remedy was a simple one. 'Go to such and such a house, take what you find under the churn, and burn it.' Sometimes a more elaborate ritual was required. One story tells of a wise woman – her name was Siobhán Grogan and she lived on the border between Limerick and Kerry – being summoned to the help of an afflicted dairy. First she had to get half a pint of whiskey, which she drank undiluted 'without taking the jug from her lips'. Then she fell to the floor in a fit and remained for some time stretched out stiff and pale as death. When life and activity returned, she sprang up and bustled about giving orders that the churning should begin. She called for the soc of a plough and had it put to heat on a good turf fire on the kitchen hearth. Meanwhile the churning was giving no results in spite of most strenuous work by the mistress and the dairymaids. ''Tis time now,' quoth Siobhán, 'and let ye all be watching that house up there on the brow of the hill', and with that she thrust the red-hot plough-iron into the churn. And sure enough the woman of the house on the brow of the hill was to be seen – and heard – running from her own door, screaming 'Stop it! Ye have the guts roasted on me! I'll make it all up to ye if ye'll stop burning me!' thus all was made clear; Siobhán was well rewarded for her trouble, and a fervent promise of no further interference, together with two firkins of good butter, assuaged the injured parties. But we hear of another case which did not turn out so well, when a farmer who lived down near the Shannon was sent by his wife to consult the famous wise woman of Clare,

Biddy Early. He was to take a sample of butter from the churn, and she would say what should be done. But his wife could not refrain from fulfilling the old custom that no food must leave the house without its pinch of salt, and she put a tiny pinch in the sample of butter unknown to her husband and the wise woman did not even have to see the sample, for before he had time to unwrap it she told him that he could be on his way home again; there was salt in the butter, and so it could not be used for any kind of magic, good or bad. It was said that Biddy Early had a most powerful charm to prevent butter stealing – the dried hand of a murderer who had been hanged in public. With this gruesome relic she would stir the cream in the churn from which the butter was being 'taken', and you knew at once from the enormous return from that churning how much butter had been spirited away from your dairy.

People had no doubt at all as to where the power to do these things came from. A common belief held that the one who wished to get these powers must invoke the devil while Mass was being celebrated, and must be ready to deliver over his or her own soul in exchange. But others maintained that they came from the fairies, and that the proper way to get them was to crawl naked under a brier, both ends of which were rooted, on May morning and then to wash all over in the dew. Whether from the devil or not, the ordinary countryman or woman had a horror of all such doings, and the general sentiment was 'I'd much rather 'twould be done to me than that I'd do it to another.' And many people who suspected that charms were being set upon their work or their property would rather endure the loss than invoke the help of counter-spells. The prayers and blessing of a holy priest were held to be stronger than any charm or spell and were often requested as remedy.

Gain, we are told, was the usual motive behind all this setting of charms and spells; it was a form of stealing without trouble or much risk of discovery. And milk and butter were not the only things threatened, for a spell could be cast upon growing crops, so that a neighbour's potato-garden gave little return while the ridges of the charm-setter were bursting with fine potatoes at digging time. Or matters could be so arranged that the cows sickened and died or that the calves were stillborn or puny while the evildoer's cattle increased and flourished. In our part of the country the charm to steal crops consisted of a number of hens' eggs hidden in the victim's garden or haggard, while that to deprive a man of the increase of his cattle was a large piece of fresh meat similarly concealed. If such things were found on the land they must be destroyed with care. First they must be taken up and carried away so that no fragment remained behind; especial care must be taken not to break the eggs. Then they must be burned in a fire on a public place such as the roadway; in this way the charm could fall on nobody in particular. There were other charms and spells which were aimed, out of pure malice, at injuring another in his person or his property without any material gain to the perpetrator. Foremost amongst these was the evil eye, the possessor of which could turn milk sour or cause crops to fail or animals to die or deprive a child of a year's growth or an adult of health or strength with a glance. The only remedy was to force the person responsible to say a prayer asking God's blessing on the afflicted person or thing. And, strange to relate, one could have the evil eye without knowing it. There was the tale of the priest and his servant boy driving along together and looking at a cow in the field. The cow fell down as they passed by. 'Look what you've done,' said the priest. And back they both went and stood over the cow, and the boy prayed fervently that God might save and bless it, without result. But scarcely had the priest said 'God bless it!' when the cow stood up as healthy as ever, for it was the priest who had the *síol trom* unknown to himself. Ever afterwards he was careful to say 'God bless it!' to every animal on which he looked.

Worst of all were the tales of attempts to murder by charms and spells. If we heard the story of the skull once, we heard it twenty times. Once upon a time, it said, there were two brothers and a sister living on a farm, and the farm next to theirs was owned by a young boy, a nephew of their own. And they determined to get that farm and join it to their own. Off went one of the men to consult Siobhán Grogan, and before he could say a single word of explanation she said 'Go you to the place of skulls and take one skull from it. And scrape the moss from it into a saucepan of milk while you're saying the name of the one that should die. And give him the milk to drink. And before a month is out you'll see what you'll see.' And – god save us all from the like – didn't they do it with a skull they took from the window of the old church. But it was back on themselves it came, for the three of them were dead from one thing or another before the year was out, and the boy they wanted to kill got their farm as well as his own, and 'twas no trouble to him with his two farms to get the finest girl in the county and their great-grandchildren are in the place yet! There was always the danger, it seems, that the spell might recoil on those who worked it, so that, between one thing and another only a very depraved person would dabble in these horrible rites.

Belief in these *piséogs* still lingers in some places, but even the memory of them is passing away now. The coming of the creameries put an end to the fear of butter stealing, while one or two recently reported cases of the laying of charms on crops have been shown to be the work of practical jokers trying to frighten credulous people. In their time, nevertheless, these things must have been the cause of grief and of terror to many, and their passing away is nothing but a blessing.

❖ GHOSTS

Everybody's grandmother has seen a ghost, says the proverb, but very few of us, their grandchildren, have been similarly visited. Nor, indeed, do most of us wish to meet visitors from the other world, having enough on our hands already with the inhabitants of this, and even those of us who proclaim most strongly our utter lack of belief in ghosts will hesitate to put the matter to the test by visiting reputedly haunted places at midnight. Many of us, in dark and lonely places, have had the uncomfortable feeling that we are 'not alone', like the man in the poem who on a lonely road did walk in fear and dread and having once turned around walked on and turned no more his head because he knew a frightful fiend did close behind him tread. Or the other poet whose lament runs:

> The other night upon the stair
> I met a man who wasn't there.
> He wasn't there again today.
> I wish that man would go away!

However, not all ghosts are formidable. Take the case of the woman who was visited by the spirit of her former husband, a poor wretch whom twenty years of marriage with a virago had finally driven to suicide. She fixed the ghost with a beady eye and said, 'I thought you'd had enough!', and the miserable being fled back into the shades. Or the honest man who woke one night to find a black shape bending over him. He waited a while. The shape made no move or sound. 'You'll excuse me,' he said, 'but I have me day's work before me tomorrow, and I never heard that your crowd were much troubled with work. So, if you don't mind, I'll go back to sleep for myself' – and with that he turned over and left the shape completely at a loss as to what to do next. Of course, not everybody can take these uninvited guests so coolly and the presence of even the mildest-mannered ghost can be a bit of a strain at times.

It is told in County Kilkenny that a poor simple boy, when passing the churchyard at night, used to stop and spend a while leaning on the gate conversing with a ghost (whom nobody else could see). The misplaced sense of humour of some local hobble-dehoys led them to attempt to frighten him, so one of them stood inside the gate, wrapped in a white sheet and moaning dismally. Along came poor Johnny and stopped at the gate as usual for his little chat. 'Bedad, that's queer,' says he. 'There's two of ye here tonight.'

The popular belief is that a ghost never comes back without a good reason. One story tells of a priest of a religious order who had come to give a mission in a remote parish, and who was sitting up late to read his office when he noticed the ghostly figure of a priest in old-fashioned clothes pointing, without saying a word, to an old book on a shelf. When the apparition vanished the priest took the old book and examined it, and found in the back of the cover a paper on which was written in faded ink, 'Confession, to be destroyed' – apparently the confession of some dumb person. Enquires next morning told him that the ghost had been seen by many in the past, but no one had had the courage to watch and see what it would do. Another similar and even more common tale is that of the ancient church ruin where lights were seen at night. A brave fellow went there to investigate and saw a priest, vested for mass, standing before the broken altar. The apparition turned and spoke, 'Will anyone serve my mass?' and the listener came forward and served the mass. When it was finished the ghost told him that he had died leaving a mass unsaid, and had to return night after night down the centuries until a living human being could witness the mass being said; now that the condition was fulfilled his spirit could rest in peace.

At Casadh na Gráige, a lonely spot on the road from Dunquin to Ballyferriter, a ghost used to sit on a large rock and terrify the passers-by. She said nothing and did nothing, just sat there, a horrid-looking old woman puffing a large pipe. The people avoided the place, taking a roundabout way over the rocks. Until one night a man from Paróiste Múrach, who had shared a bottle of Dutch Courage with some cronies in Dunquin, was passing that way, and full of bravado and the craving for a smoke he accosted the ghost and asked for a puff of the pipe. He took a few good puffs and handed it back with the conventional prayer 'May the Lord have mercy on the souls of your dead!' The ghost handed it back and he smoked again and prayed again. And again a third time. Then the ghost spoke; she was a poor travelling woman who had died there long ago and her body was not found and no one had uttered a prayer for her repose, until now when his prayer had released her from her long vigil. She gave him the pipe, promising him that as long as he kept the whole thing a secret the pipe would always remain full of tobacco, no matter how often he smoked. For a couple of months he enjoyed it, but like so many more, he could not keep his mouth shut, and so the spell was broken and he was left with an old clay pipe, cold and empty.

Another unfortunate victim of circumstance was the ghost that haunted a little old postern gate on the road between Rathkeale and Ardagh; this was the spirit of a poor girl who was betrayed and murdered by a local landlord. After the fall of dark no horse would walk on the roadway in front of the gate where the blood had been shed. When a horse baulked there you had to spread straw or a rug or a few sacks on the road, and the horse went on. Many still alive remember seeing this, but the postern was built up and the roadway renewed and so the ghost was laid to rest.

There are many spirits condemned to haunt lonely places because of their own crimes, and for these we have little sympathy. Talking to them does not help; we can do nothing to shorten their punishment. Not far from Drogheda, close to the river Boyne, a weird drumming sound may be heard on certain dark nights. This is the earthbound spirit of the miscreant who stole St Patrick's goat, an animal of merry disposition which not only provided milk for the saint but also kept him amused by its tricks and pranks, and St Patrick got both pleasure and profit from it until the sad morning when the goat was gone, leaving only a cut spancel behind. High and low they searched, but the poor creature was already converted into goat soup and devoured by the greedy thief. Not only that, but he had the effrontery to make a drum of the skin and beat a rousing tattoo on it to show his opinion of the saint; but saints are only human and Patrick loosed a curse upon him, so that he became a witless wanderer playing his shameful drum from door to door and living on the scraps the housewives gave him. Even after the close of his ill-spent life there was no release; his spirit still drums dolefully along the Boyne as a solemn warning to all who may cast covetous glances upon clergymen's goats.

Another County Limerick ghost made a brief appearance in fulfilment of a rash promise. It was in the bad old days when the priest hunters were abroad, and a kindly landlord, Viscount Southwell, gave shelter in his house to a hunted priest. The son of the house, a freethinker, had many an argument with the priest about the existence of an afterlife. 'Look you, reverend sir,' quoth he 'if there be another world, and if I get there first, I shall return and give you testimony of it.' The young man went on his travels to France and the priest continued to call at the big house, until one night as he sat alone, writing, a white hand was laid on the table beside him, a hand bearing a ring which he recognised. No word was said, but when the hand was drawn away its print was seen burned deep into the tabletop where it remained for over a hundred and fifty years. It was a month after this apparition that the news came that the young man had been killed in a duel in Paris on the very evening that his ghost had fulfilled the rash promise made to the priest.

In many parts of Ireland the story is told of a brave servant boy who volunteered to stay the night in a haunted house. The old landlord had come to the end of his evil days without revealing where his hoard was hidden, and his ghost was seen frequently, a fearsome sight which struck terror into all. But the brave boy agreed to spend a night in the old house and came fortified with two bottles, one of holy water and the other of whiskey. Late in the night he was dozing before the fire when his eye caught a movement, and there was the figure in the big picture of the old reprobate stepping out of the canvas on to the sideboard and down on the floor. Slowly the figure approached, its evil stare fixed unblinkingly on the bottles. With a swift and practised movement it raised one of them to its lips – and vanished with a blue flash and a loud crackle, leaving only a smell of brimstone behind. It had drunk from the wrong bottle. And there next morning, as proof positive, was the empty space in the canvas, and more than that, there behind it was a cavity in the wall full of bags of gold, the old scoundrel's hoard. As we might expect, the brave boy got his share of the gold, and married his master's pretty daughter as the reward of the courage.

Then there was the case of Damer of the prodigious wealth who started life as a poor struggling sort of a fellow until chance brought to his house a suave gentleman richly clad in black, whose origin was betrayed only by an occasional whiff of sulphur or a glimpse of a cloven hoof. Damer's soul, no less, is what he wanted, and in return he was ready to hand over a riding boot full of gold. 'Done!' said Damer, and a night was fixed for the payment. Damer had provided an extra large boot, but the dark gentleman poured in without hesitation first one and then a second sack of golden guineas. But, behold! the boot was as empty as ever, and the astonished visitor from below had to hurry off for another couple of sackfuls, but to no avail. The boot was not yet full. And so the night went on. The dark gentleman getting more and more hot and bothered, his clothes torn and dusty and his brow furrowed and dripping sweat, and more than a hundred sacks of guineas vanished into the boot. Then came the dawn when he had to return below and leave Damer to go down to the cellar, now full of the gold that had poured through the boot which had stood soleless over a hole in the floor, where he revived his gold-shovelling workmen with glasses of good whiskey and rewarded each of them with the full of his hat of guineas, thoughtfully refraining from any mention of the few they had pocketed in the course of their labours.

Some ghosts appear to give warning of future events. It is told of Dr Ussher, Protestant archbishop of Armagh, who like Fr O'Flynn was famous for learning and wisdom and piety, that a lady who was dead appeared to him and invited him to come to supper with her on the following night; he accepted the invitation, and never took supper again in this life, for he died the following afternoon, and so was able to keep his ghostly appointment.

Ghost stories abound on all sides. Of helpful ghosts and harmful ones, of ghosts malicious and ghosts friendly. Some of them taken up with their own woes, others with kindly message for the living. Still others with evil intent. Everybody's grandmother has seen as least one, and the average person is still quite happy to leave it rest at that and seek no closer contact with them.

❖ Sunken Cities

In the old days, before Columbus sailed to the west, Ireland stood out on the very uttermost edge of the known world. Even in ancient times there had been coming and going to Britain, to Europe and to places beyond; soldiers, merchants and seas captains, missionaries, minstrels, pirates and pilgrims all had sailed across the narrow seas and brought word of the lands that lay towards the rising sun. Even the eastern world, Baghdad and Hindustan and Cathay were not unknown in the travellers' tales. But to the west there was nothing except the boundless ocean and the men who loved along the Atlantic coasts were full of wonder as to what might lie out there below the horizon. Such a vacuum could not be tolerated, and the storytellers' imagination was not lacking in filling it with wonderful accounts of magic lands and of cities sunken under the waves.

These tales were not entirely imaginary. Hardy men had sailed out into the sea and some had returned. Foremost among them were the early monks and hermits seeking solitude, and the rocky islands along our west coast from Sceilig Mhichíl to Tory still hold the remains of their cells and oratories. We know that they reached the Faroe Islands and Iceland, and they may have been the first Europeans to see Greenland and the north-eastern fringes of America. And if these grave and holy men could tell of marvels such as the whales and the walruses, the volcanoes and the icebergs why should the stories of sea serpents and floating islands and undersea meadows not be believed too? Further fire for the popular imagination was provided by the mirages which may still be seen at times from the west coast, and for which we have the testimony of such reliable witnesses as the well-known scholar and antiquary Thomas Johnson Westropp who saw it three times and even made a coloured sketch of it:

It was a clear evening, with a fine golden sunset, when, just as the sun went down, a dark island suddenly appeared far out to sea, but not on the horizon. It had two hills, one wooded; between these, from a low plain, rose towers and curls of smoke. My mother, brother, and several friends saw it at the same time; one person cried that he could see New York!

With such material to work upon the storytellers produced a whole series of tales. Some of these are preserved in our ancient literature and many have survived in the traditions of the people who live by the sea. Of the old tales none was better or more widely known that the Voyage of St Brendan which spread far beyond Ireland, and in which the matter-of-fact chronicle of the sea-faring monks was later elaborated to include a whale so large that the travellers, thinking it was an island, landed there to celebrate the feast of Easter, and a giant iceberg upon which Judas Iscariot was permitted to spend one day in each year as solace from the eternal fire. Then there is the story of Maelduin who sailed out with chosen companions to find his father's murderers. Their boat was swept out into the great ocean by a storm and they came to many wonderful islands. On one of these were ants as large as young horses, on another a herd of red-hot pigs came out of caves all day long but returned to their dens at night so that voyagers, led by flocks of birds, could land and feast upon magic fruit. On still another was a mighty beast which turned around inside its own skin, or tiring of this curious exercise, stood still while its skin revolved around it with great speed, a circumstance which discouraged the voyagers from landing there. In another land horrible giants raced fearsome horses. In other islands they were feasted and entertained and saw fountains of milk and wine or were received by beautiful women. They saw a fair country, full of people and cattle, under the sea, and were horrified when a huge serpent carried off a cow. They came to great silver pillars standing in the water and cut off a fragment of a silver veil to carry home as an offering to the church. Finally, in a far distant islet they met a holy hermit who told them to return to Ireland where they should find the murderers, but they must forgive them in thanksgiving to God for their safety.

Another ancient sea story recounts how Bran Mac Feabhaill and his twenty-seven followers set sail to the west in search of a land of which a fairy woman had sung. After seeing many marvels they came at last to the Land of Lovely Women and were so well entertained by these fair ladies that centuries passed unnoticed. When at last they returned to Ireland they saw that all had changed and were horrified when the first man sprang ashore and crumbled into ashes; the others learned the truth from those on shore, and told their story from the boat and then sailed out again into the unknown. It was to this land of sunlight and flowers, of endless youth and love that Connla, son of Conn of the Hundred Battles, was enticed by the fairy maiden and was never seen again. It was there that Oisín was brought by Niamh of the Golden Hair, daughter of the king of that country with many names, the Land of the Youth, the Plain of Flowers, the Country of the Living, the Island of Promise, and after three hundred years that seemed to pass as quickly as three Oisín returned to find all his friends gone and only an old tradition of the Fianna and its mighty warriors, to become an old man and recount his tales to St Patrick who had them written down that they might not be lost.

Around the shores of the North Sea much of the land lies very low, some of it under sea level and protected from inundation by great dykes. We remember the dreadful storm early in 1953 when the dykes broke and great stretches of country in Holland were flooded, and parts of eastern England, Belgium and Friesland were under water too. There were worse disasters in the past, such as that of the year 1421 when the Dutch dykes broke and seventy-two villages were swept away with the loss of over a hundred thousand people. The dykes were mended and most of the land won back from the sea, but all along those coasts there still are traditions of farms, churches and whole towns taken by the sea and never won back. Here in Ireland we have our traditions of the 'lost town of Bannow' on the south coast of County Wexford, where it is said, a whole town was swallowed up by the waves and the drifting sand, and where part of the ruins may still be seen. Other stories of lost cities along the south coast may have less historical basis, but may hold a memory of some ancient catastrophe; this might also be true of the 'round towers of other days' under the waters of Lough Neagh. Strangest of all are the legends of fields and towns under the sea off the west coast.

We are told that a ship's captain sailing out of Limerick gave passage to a young man, and that somewhere off the north shore of the Dingle peninsula the passenger remarked that he had come to the end of his journey, that his home was in a town under the water at that point, and with an airy salutation he jumped overboard and sank out of sight. Some time later the ship's captain, back in Limerick, could not help staring at the same young man one night in a tavern, whereupon the young man, remarking that some people see more than is good for them, thrust his fingers into the poor captain's eyes and blinded him. The tale is corroborated by the evidence of one Diarmaid O'Shea, a fisherman of those parts who ran into a bank of fog while out alone in his *naemhóg* pulling lobster pots and was amazed to see an island where none should be. He landed and walked through flowering meadows to a splendid house, where he found an old man and a beautiful young girl surrounded by all sorts of wealth and fine furniture. 'Welcome, welcome, Diarmaid O'Shea' said the old man, 'We have been waiting long for you, because you are to take the most beautiful thing in the house for yourself!' Poor Diarmaid was dazed by the beauty of everything, and small blame to him when he had never seen the hundredth part of such riches. He looked about him and finally spoke. 'You're very kind, sir, and if 'tis no harm I'll take that lovely gold cup. Won't my mother be out of her mind with pride and she drinking tea out of it and all the neighbours envying her?' 'Oh you fool, you stupid boy! Is it blind you are not to know beauty? Take your cup and go, and make no delay on your road!' Poor Diarmaid snatched the cup and ran for his boat – and gained the shore only just in time to escape the great wave that swept after him. But he was troubled in his mind and asked advice from a wise old priest. 'You are the lucky man to escape. What the old man meant was his daughter, that you should stay and marry her. And if you did that, you'd never see Kerry again, no, nor Heaven either. I'm thinking! And now, throw that cup back to those that gave it to you!' Diarmaid went to the top of the highest cliff and threw the cup into the sea, and peace came back to his mind.

In Dingle Bay there is a city which rises over the waves once in every seven years, and has been seen, we are told, by many people. A similar tale from Aran speaks of 'Beag-Arainn', the lovely island which appears once every five years. If one could land on it and kindle a fire, the island would become fixed and solid, and if anyone doubts this, is it not a related fact that Inishbofin, off the west coast of County Galway, was disenchanted in this way by fishermen who went on shore carrying live coals in an iron pot? In west Clare they tell of 'Cill Stuithín'. Some say it lies off Loop Head, others that it is near Mutton Island in Mal Bay. Its golden roofs and towers shine clear under the water, and the scent of its flowery fields rises to tantalise the fishermen passing over it. But it is well not to tarry long in admiration, for its inhabitants have the unpleasant custom of raising storms to drive away the over-curious. It was once dry land, but was drowned in the sea with all its people by magic, but hidden somewhere in County Clare is a golden key, and when that key is found the city will rise again in all its beauty, to be – who knows? – one of our foremost seaside resorts.

An honest man of County Galway, one Murrogh O'Lee, was about his lawful occasions on the high seas west of that county when he came upon an island where he landed and was entertained. As a parting gift he was given a book, and on coming home and opening it he found that it contained the cure for every known illness. He set up as a doctor and won great fame for his cures, and his sons and his sons' sons followed him in that craft, so that the name of the O'Lee physicians was famed throughout the land. The precious book was saved and may still be seen in the library of the Royal Irish Academy in Dublin and he who can read it may still work wondrous cures. In actual fact the book is a medical treatise of the middle ages, bearing the date 1434, and the medical family of O'Lee (the name means descendants of the physician) had practised the healing arts from ancient times. But why spoil a good story – which we may be sure did no harm to the family – by too exact details of this kind?

There are other sunken cities off the shores of Mayo and Donegal and Antrim. One of them appears to the north of Erris, and if one person lives to see it three times it will lose its magic and become solid land. Another, off Inishowen, is rather exclusive, as it may only be seen by a descendant of princely family of the O'Dohertys of Inishown. The others however, from 'Tún Tóime' off south-west Kerry to 'Tír Hiúdi' near Tory Island, may be seen by anybody lucky enough to be in the right place at the right time, and may be freed from their spells to form a rich patrimony for those who know the workings of magic.

All through the middle ages and even into early modern times the makers of maps and charts were at pains to include the islands of legend in their works. Hy Brasil and St Brendan's Isle, Dathuli Island and the Green Island appear plainly marked on the maps of the time. More than one expedition was fitted out to find them, and as late as 1674 a certain Captain John Nisbet, sailing out of Killybegs for France, brought home a wonderful tale of how he had landed on Hy Brasil and rescued an old Scots gentleman and his retainers who had long been held captive there. Christopher Columbus had studied the old maps and heard the old tales before he set out to find islands as strange as any in the legends, and we need not be surprised to hear that among his crew was one 'William of Galway, an Irishman' who, we may be sure, supplied any missing details in his admiral's knowledge of the magic islands of the great ocean.

❖ BLACK CAT AND BROOMSTICK

As a small boy on summer holidays in County Clare a solitary ramble brought me to a little one-roomed house wherein lived alone an old, old woman. To me she was quite friendly although I could understand little of her mumblings, and with childhood's direct approach I remarked, 'You have only two teeth, ma'am,' to which she replied, ''tis true for you and sure, *a mhaoineach*, and what harm if they were opposite one another! And sure I have the false ones that belonged to Big Jim Kinirey until the guns swelled on him, but I could never make much of a hand on them, except that they're great for printing a pattern on the top of an apple-cake, and by the same token you'll have to eat a pointer of the last one I made, and not take the luck out of the house on me.' Luckily, in the matter of the apple-cake, a youthful appetite takes little heed either of the unconventional modes of decoration or of slight hardening due to age, for I learned that old Nellie might have taken offence at refusal, and had the habit of calling down frightful curses on those who displeased her. This habit was not without advantage to her, for the neighbours placated her with donations of milk, vegetables and the apples that went into her apple-cake. She, on her side, had some skill in herbal cures, and never refused her recipes to those who approached her with due deference.

On my way home that day I couldn't help thinking that the old lady was very like the witch in the storybooks; the black cat in the hearth and the heather besom behind the door were just what a witch should have, and when I heard of her cures and her curses my suspicions grew. But I soon found out that the classic figure of the witch cleaving the night air on a broomstick with her cat perched on the pillion was not recognised in local tradition. Old Nellie might be a *bean feasa*, skilled in cures and in divination, or even an old *cailleach* who stole the cows' milk disguised as a hare, but not a witch; luckily for old Nellie and for many another of her like, the type of witch so feared, hated and persecuted in Britain and Europe in former times has no part in Irish tradition.

From the middle ages up to the middle of the eighteenth century the belief in witches was common in Britain and Europe, and not merely among simple people but also among the wise and the learned. Belief that magic power is held by certain individuals is common all over the world, but the witch mania claimed that there was an organised society of witches working evil in the community. It was held that both men and women, both young and old, belonged to this society and that it met in groups to do its foul work. Each member had made a bargain with the devil, selling his or her soul in return for membership and the power that went with it. Each member had been admitted to the society with horrible rites and ceremonies which mocked and blasphemed the Christian ritual; the devil presided over these in person. And each member was given a 'familiar spirit', a demon in the shape of an animal – often a black cat – or appearing as a deformed human being. In return for this the witch became expert in all forms of evil magic. The witch had the power to raise storms, to bring blight on the crops and disease on the cattle, to cure people by transferring their ailments to others, to kill or maim by making an image of the victim and stabbing or burning it, and to concoct all sorts of poisons and spells. By smearing a broomstick with a magic ointment the witch could fly through the air upon it with great speed, and thus they travelled to their dreadful conferences.

Many leaders of both church and state firmly believed in all this and held, too, that the witches were a dreadful menace to both church and state, a threat to be wiped out at all costs. Learned men wrote books on the subject, telling of the danger, showing how witches might be recognised and calling upon the authorities to suppress witchcraft. Indeed there is much evidence to show that groups of people (whether wicked or merely deluded is hard to say) did actually carry out rites and ceremonies associated with witchcraft. As a result of all this the fear of witches and the consequent persecution of suspects spread into almost every country in Europe, and many hundreds of people were arrested, examined in various ways including horrible tortures, tried and condemned to death or imprisonment, and many others were driven away from their homes or even killed by mobs of terrified people. Laws against witches were solemnly passed through parliaments, for instance in England under Henry VIII. James VI of Scotland, who became king of England after the death of Elizabeth, took a personal interest in the suppression of witchcraft and wrote a book condemning it. Under the Commonwealth there were organised witch hunts, and rewards were paid for the discovery of witches; unscrupulous persons or those with scores to settle took advantage of this and denounced many unfortunates, most of them undoubtedly innocent, and handed them over to torture and death. The most notorious witch-finder in England was one Matthew Hopkins who made quite a business of it, reaping a substantial harvest of rewards. He had suspects pricked with pins to find the 'witch spot', made them repeat prayers rapidly without a mistake, had them tied up and thrown into a pond to see if they would float or sink. Many poor creatures failed in the tests and so were condemned, until somebody got the bright idea of testing the brave Matthew himself, and when he failed to pass the tests he was himself accused of witchcraft and executed. These extravagances led to second thoughts on the matter of witchcraft, and gradually the terror died out. In 1736 the laws against witchcraft were abolished in Britain.

There are, however, a few instances of witch hunts in Ireland which show us what might have happened here, too, if the temper and traditions of the ordinary people had been different from what they were. The most famous of these is the case of Alice Keteler and her companions in Kilkenny in the year 1324. At that time the bishop of Ossory was Richard Ledrede, an Englishman who had been appointed to the diocese in 1317. It was reported to him that witches were at work and it was alleged that Dame Alice and her companions had given up the practice of Christianity and now made sacrifices of black cocks and other creatures to the devil; that they assembled at crossroads and other unhallowed places and brewed foul mixtures of the entrails of the sacrificed beasts, with herbs, insects, hair and nails of dead men and unbaptised children; that Dame Alice had been married four times, and that she had killed three of her husbands – William Outlaw, Adam Blund and Richard Wall – by spells, and had by poison and incantations reduced her present husband, John de Paor, to a state of physical and mental collapse; and finally that she had a familiar spirit named Robin the son of Art who appeared under the various forms of a cat, a black dog or a negro, often accompanied by other spirits in various shapes. It was also stated that she had been seen on dark nights sweeping the streets towards the house of her son, William Outlaw, and repeating charms with the intention of drawing all the wealth of the town to him:

> To the house of William my son
> Hie all the wealth of Kilkenny town!

Straightaway the bishop ordered the arrest of Dame Alice, but she had friends in high position, and the civil authorities informed the bishop that she could not be imprisoned unless she had been formally accused of witchcraft and heresy and excommunicated by the church. While this and other legal matters were being unravelled, Dame Alice slipped away to Dublin, and later when the hunt was up again she took ship to England and out of our story. The bishop tried to proceed against her son, William Outlaw, but found his course hindered by William's friends and was even thrown into prison himself. Complicated legal proceedings followed, but at last the bishop triumphed; Dame Alice had escaped but her companions were brought to trial and some of them, after confession under torture, were executed by being burned at the stake, while William Outlaw and his friends did public penance for their opposition to the bishop. This is the only known case of a witch trial in Ireland before the Reformation, and that this apparent freedom from witchcraft was really the case and is not merely due to the loss of the old records is shown by a declaration of the Parliament held in Trim, County Meath, in 1447, in which the king, Henry VI, was assured that the black art of sorcery was unknown in the land of Ireland. Even laws against witchcraft seem to have been unknown in Ireland, for we learn in the next instance of a witch trail, held in 1578, that the judges on coming to Kilkenny found the jails so full that they held trials immediately, and had thirty-six people executed, among whom were two witches and a blackamoor who tried 'according to the natural law for that we found no law to try them by in this realm'. Apparently the unfortunate negro was also accused of witchcraft, and it is to be feared that his dark colour was taken as a sign of his dabbling in black magic. However, under Elizabeth this lack in the law was remedied, and full-blown laws against witchcraft were put on the statute books in 1586; these remained in force until about a hundred and fifty years ago, but even when the witch hunt was raging in Britain the Irish laws found little work to do.

We must go on to 1661 for the next record of a witch trial, this time in Youghal, where an old woman named Florence Newton was accused of afflicting a girl named Mary Longdon with fits and trances, causing her to vomit pins, needles, nails, straw, wool and other matters and to be thrown out of bed and into attics and cupboards. The old woman was cast into prison, and while there was further accused of causing the death of one David Jones by spells. She was tested by having to repeat the Lord's Prayer and by being stuck with pins and awls, but the record of the verdict and sentence are lost, and we do not know what happened to poor old Florence. Of the last recorded trial in Ireland, we know more. This was at Carrickfergus in 1711, where seven women were accused of persecuting a clergyman's widow and her friends and servants; one of these ladies declared that she recognised the accused as her tormentors. Much evidence was given about pains and fits, apparitions, throwing of stones at windows, clothing and bedlinen flung about and so forth. In the end the accused were found guilty on evidence that certainly would not be accepted today, and condemned to a year's imprisonment and exposure in the pillory. They were lucky to get off so lightly.

It is interesting to note that in the records of these few Irish witch trials the names of all concerned are those of Norman, English or Scottish settlers, and the locations are the settlers' towns. The 'native Irish' and their localities do not appear at all. This is no more than we might expect from the Irish tradition, in which there was plenty of foolish belief and peculiar custom but not that organised form of witchcraft and witch-hunting which brought so much grief and sorrow in other lands.

MERCIER PRESS

IRISH PUBLISHER - IRISH STORY

We hope you enjoyed this book.

Since 1944, Mercier Press has published books that have been critically important to Irish life and culture. Books that dealt with subjects that informed readers about Irish scholars, Irish writers, Irish history and Ireland's rich heritage.

We believe in the importance of providing accessible histories and cultural books for all readers and all who are interested in Irish cultural life.

Our website is the best place to find out more information about Mercier, our books, authors, news and the best deals on a wide variety of books. Mercier tracks the best prices for our books online and we seek to offer the best value to our customers, offering free delivery within Ireland.

Sign up on our website or complete and return the form below to receive updates and special offers.

www.mercierpress.ie
www.facebook.com/mercier.press
www.twitter.com/irishpublisher

- -

Name:

Email:

Address:

Mercier Press, Unit 3b, Oak House, Bessboro Rd, Blackrock, Cork, Ireland